Music & Ministry

Music & Ministry

A Biblical Counterpoint

SECOND EDITION

CALVIN M. JOHANSSON

© 1984, 1998 by Hendrickson Publishers, Inc.
P. O. Box 3473
Peabody, Massachusetts 01961–3473
All rights reserved.
First edition 1984
Second edition 1998
Printed in the United States of America

Second Printing — July 2001

Library of Congress Cataloging-in-Publication Data

Johansson, Calvin M.
  Music & ministry: a biblical counterpoint / Calvin M.
Johansson. — 2nd ed.
  Includes bibliographic references and index.
  ISBN 1-56563-361-X (pbk.)
  1. Church music. 2. Music—Philosophy and aesthetics.
3. Music—Religious aspects—Christianity. 4. Bible—Theology.
I. Title.
ML3869.J63 1998
264′.2′01—dc21   98-19453
                                                      CIP
                                                      MN

*Dedicated to the teaching ministry
of the church musician*

Table of Contents

Prologue   ix

1 Philosophical Perspectives   1
Aestheticism   2
Pragmatism   4
Biblical Counterpoint   7

2 The Doctrine of Creation   8
Creation, Dependence, and Independence   8
The Natural World and Form   10
Creatio Continua and the Church   12
Creativity   17
Church Nurture of Creativity   19
Summary: Creative Worth and a Church Imperative   22

3 The Imago Dei   27
The Broad Imago Dei   28
The Narrow Imago Dei   32
Summary: Musical Imaging   36

4 The Incarnation   39
Pastoral Humility and Love   40
Communication: Relevance   44
Communication: Form and Content   50
Implicit Communication   52
Summary   54

5 The Gospel and Contemporary Culture   56
Gospel Characteristics   57
Pop Culture   62
The Church and Pop Culture   66

Pop Music Characteristics   67
The Church and Pop Music   76
Truth and Methods   80
Folk Music and Jazz   81
Summary and an Urgent Theological Resolve   85

6   **Faith**   87
The Wholeness of the Christian Life   87
Intellectual and Emotional Imbalances in Church Music   94
Faith Action and Tendency Gratification   99
Summary and Congregational Methodology   104

7   **Stewardship**   106
Motivations for Stewardship   106
Stewardship's Scope   108
Doing One's Best—Principle One   110
Some Dangers   112
Growth—Principle Two   115
Church Music Education   119
A Contrapuntal Stewardship   121

8   **Mystery and Awe**   123
Music and Mystery   125
Truth and Musical Composition   127
Beyond the Explicitness of Words   133
Imparting a Sense of Mystery   135
Summary   136

9   **Conclusion**   138
The Crucifixion   138
The Resurrection   141
A Contrapuntal Dynamic   145
Application   151

Notes   169
Bibliography   179
Index   187

Prologue

Of necessity, church musicians are zealous, energetic workers who have little time for reflection, contemplation, and philosophic thought. They generally seek practical things: new repertoire, problem-solving strategies, performance helps, and the latest trends in designing and conducting worship.

Yet here is a book that asks music directors, pastors, singers, instrumentalists, organists, and pianists to set aside their music making momentarily and reflect seriously on their activities—to take a brief sabbatical for reviewing biblical principles foundational to music ministry.

Such reflection is important: thinking determines doing. The music director's philosophy of ministry will affect many choices that must be made. What genres of music will be used for congregational singing? What pieces will be selected for the choirs and instrumental ensembles? What choirs and other ensembles will be offered? Which musical styles, from a burgeoning plurality of possibilities, will be included? Which worldview will form the basis for the ministry's musical standards? What will be the aesthetic and theological depth of the music chosen?

As we face a new millennium, the importance of finding a solid foundation for church music is greater than ever. Many have observed that the twentieth century has largely stripped church music of meaningful standards. Such a state is most unfortunate since church music purports to represent a Judeo-Christian value system, a system steeped in absolutes and objective standards.

The prevailing worldview, which makes truth relative and denies the existence of absolutes, is becoming the new philosophical basis for church music.[1] Its emphasis on individual liberty, taken to radical extremes, along with a sweeping cultural egalitarianism and pluralism, has led musicians, church leaders, and congregations to believe that all music, regardless of style or quality, is equally valid in the church. This expanded subjectivism does away with biblical standards by which music might be rated as good, bad, better, and best, and substitutes taste as the arbiter of value. Consequently, many people think that there are as many shades of musical virtue and value as there are individuals. In essence, anything goes! However, such a belief tends toward the absurd and is out of synch with the biblical record. It needs to be addressed.

Music and Ministry: A Biblical Counterpoint speaks to these issues. Its working premise is that the only thing that retains some vestige of authority for Christians in our culture is the Word of God. Dialogue concerning musical standards will ultimately fail if predicated upon suppositions arising from the relativistic spirit of our age.

Remarkably, the Word shows us a ministry approach that is at once accommodative and prescriptive. It is true that one does not save the world by giving it a warmed-over version of itself. Yet dynamic ministry takes into account people's contextual condition. At this juncture in history the church desperately needs the biblical counterpoint of being in the world yet not of the world. Musicians are to be musical prophets—not for the sake of music, but for the sake of the gospel.

A theological perspective on church music clarifies and deepens our understanding of these and all related areas. The result is a solid biblical understanding upon which to base choices. Energized and shaped by a nourishing theological repast, church music will begin to reflect divine truth.

Pastoral music ministry, as opposed to evangelistic, missionary, or other music ministries, is the field of inquiry in these pages. This is not to say that principles valid for pastoral music ministry would necessarily be invalid for other music ministries, but some emphases would change. For our purposes we shall be concerned chiefly with the music program of the local church—the pastoral ministry of music.

A point must now be made that is critical to understanding this book: its various chapters and sections begin from different theological doctrines and topics and arrive at differing emphases and conclusions. *No single section is intended to stand alone.* Each needs the others in a contrapuntal dynamic. As in musical counterpoint, such a contrapuntal "discussion" acknowledges the right of each theological "theme" to exist independently in its own right. Yet only as these independent themes are combined will church music ministry display a full-orbed, well-rounded, and dynamic theistic worldview. What is said about creation and creativity in Chapter 2, for example, can only be understood in the light of every other chapter. This is important to remember, for then the apparent contradictions between many of these themes will be seen as illuminating the various sides of an exceedingly large and multifaceted subject. Readers who wish a further explanation of this method before beginning Chapter 1 may refer to the section of Chapter 9 called "A Contrapuntal Dynamic."

Approaching these theological topics contrapuntally (in relationship with one another, as it were) will keep one from hasty solutions that emphasize only one side of the truth. These doctrinal themes will come together in the last chapter in a counterpoint whose design will affirm integrity and practicality, shunning legalistic rules and harsh rigidity. Meanwhile, many volatile matters are dealt with in a forthright manner in accordance with the subject of the moment. No apology is made for the direct approach taken. These issues must be faced openly, honestly, and with a certain biblical ruggedness.

We proceed!

1   *Philosophical Perspectives*

Pastoral music ministry is extraordinarily rewarding. It is rewarding because it deals with basic life issues, values with eternal significance. Music directors are concerned with much more than music.

The practical working out of a church musician's calling is not as easy as it might seem. Having arrived at a set of musical standards and ministry goals, often achieved at great personal sacrifice, and after wrestling extensively with substantive cultural issues, the music director will be subject to enormous pressure to accede to the musical demands and tastes of congregations, clergy, choirs, church boards, and music committees. All too often their wishes are in direct conflict with the prophetic ministry objectives and personal conscience of the music director. It then becomes increasingly difficult to stay the course as the winds of opposing points of view batter and toss the music program about like the proverbial ship without a rudder. The whole enterprise is in danger of capsizing as it is driven along by the latest cultural squall.

The fact is that, confusion or not, Sundays roll around in a steady, unhalting procession. Choices must be made concerning the required complement of instrumental, vocal, and congregational music. Will it be Bach, Hayes, Palestrina, Hayford, Wesley, Vaughan Williams, Paris, Crosby, Williamson, or a combination of these? The choices we make reflect our thinking. One's music fleshes out one's intent. Even those who deny having any musical, theological, or philosophical value system base their decisions on some value system—even that of no system. Inevitably we choose; inevitably we judge the music we use in the light of our philosophy. The only sure defense against caprice is sound thinking. It is a critical necessity that every church musician formulate a solid underlying philosophical rationale that is coherent, comprehensive, and creative.

The key point is that the church musician must have a valid base from which to work. If we cannot avoid choices, and they are made as a result of our philosophical position (admitted or not) it is imperative that we formulate credible guiding principles. We cannot afford to be careless or indiscriminate in coming to grips with the issues. It is not a matter of having a philosophy (we all have one) or choosing what best suits our needs and the expediency of the moment. It is a matter of wrestling with the substantive alternatives until we are compelled to adopt a position that not only agrees with revealed truth but also enthusiastically promulgates that truth in all its fullness.

Aestheticism

Generally, church musicians base decisions about their programs on two philosophies: aestheticism and pragmatism. A musician who is an aestheticist will be concerned primarily with the artistic worth of church music. For example:

> The rhythm should have life and movement without levity, and dignity without heaviness. The melody of all the parts, not of the treble only, should be shapely in outline, and neither angular nor dull; in general it should be diatonic, and chromatic intervals should be only sparingly used. The harmony should be for the most part simple, avoiding excessive use of discords which introduce a note of vulgarity or triviality, and which pall with repetition.[1]

Archibald Davison, in *Protestant Church Music in America*, lists seven theoretical elements of music that must be shaped in certain ways to produce music that is free of secular associations and is good enough to use in church.[2] Naturally, artistic considerations are useful and quite necessary. But such concerns may lead to aestheticism if church music becomes its own end. A preoccupation with beauty for its own sake can lead to conceit and pride and an ungenerous desire for praise.

The problem is not the beauty of a particular piece of music but the blindness that fails to see in that music anything of transcendental value.

There are three difficulties with aestheticism as a philosophical basis for church music. First, aesthetic analysis, like music theory, comes after the fact. Artistry cannot be achieved automatically by following theoretical rules deduced from what has been done. Aesthetic insights are valuable as guideposts and are useful (depending on the particular system) as a check on musical quality, but legalistic regulations for the management of music in the church are doomed to failure. If church music is to flourish, it must have a philosophical base that goes beyond legalism.

Second, a perusal of aesthetic theories shows that as a branch of philosophy, aesthetics is concerned with explaining beauty within a given system of thought. Art is part of the reality of our world and therefore must have a place in the philosopher's system. Yet there is no way to insure that one's sensitivity to artistic values will be enhanced by an analysis of the beautiful. Many philosophers who give lengthy explanations of beauty do not have a very high personal regard for the arts. Aesthetics, then, used methodologically, cannot guarantee an improvement in musical taste and hence does little to promote musical growth and maturity. This is particularly true in a world that denies the possibility of absolutes, including aesthetic absolutes. Without the anchor of objective artistic norms, all aesthetic talk becomes only a matter of opinion. In such a climate there is no reason to take aesthetic pronouncements seriously.

A third problem with aestheticism is the danger of idolatry. An all-consuming passion for great art, first and foremost, puts God and art on the same plane. Yet leveling the playing field, as it were, is a dead end. It leads to an equality of entities that is heretical. After a lifetime of study in the field of aesthetics, DeWitt Parker, an American aesthetician, said of religion and art:

> For these stories, even when believed, have an existence in the imagination precisely comparable to that of works of art, and their influence upon sentiment is of exactly the same order. They are most effective when beautiful, as the legends of Christ and Buddha are beautiful; and

they function by the sympathetic transference of attitude from the story to the believer. Even when no longer accepted as true their influence may persist, for the values they embody lose none of their compulsion. And, although as an interpretation of life based upon faith religion is doubtless eternal, its specific forms are probably all fictitious; hence each particular religion is destined to pass from the sphere of faith to that of art. The Greek religion has long since gone there, and there also a large part of our own will someday go—what is lost for faith is retained for beauty.[3]

Charles T. Smith thought of music and religion in a similar way:

Now a church is like a theatre, and as soon as the service begins we are conscious of entering a world of illusion or make-believe in which the creed and ritual of any religion appear to be logically developed and, to that extent, satisfying to the intellect, because a religion is a work of art. It may be based upon the most incredible tenets, but if it is given good constructive form, fashioned with competent craftsmanship—which is usually the case with institutional religions which have an elaborate ritual—it is identical with an immense play . . . Religion is indeed, like music, an art; and a system of theology, like a system of music, is, as Dr. Charles Singer claims, "As much the product of human ingenuity as a motor car."[4]

In making aesthetics the foundation for a philosophy of church music, we run the risk of making art equal to God, or at least making it essential to knowing God. Aesthetic experience can provide a basis for arguing the existence of God,[5] but there can be no justification for placing art in a position where it may in effect become an object of worship. We worship the Creator, not the created—God, not beauty.

The dangers of aestheticism are clear. At best, its nebulous, analytical passivity does not strongly encourage a creative dynamic; at worst, it is idolatrous.

Pragmatism

The other philosophy that often serves as a foundation for music ministry is pragmatism. Far more prevalent than aestheticism, pragmatism enjoys a stranglehold on music ministry in many quarters of the church. It is believed that "For church music the standard must be primarily a practical one . . . good church music is that which does most effectively what it is supposed to do."[6] Function is everything.[7] Music becomes a contrivance. The overriding concern is achieving a predetermined result. This result (end) justifies the use of any music (means) as long as the anticipated result is worthy. In the ethical realm, for example, lying or stealing is thought justified when the goal is a noble one. Likewise in the artistic realm, doing away with musical goodness and truth is considered justified when the intended result is meritorious. Compositional standards become nonentities—categories that are no longer valid, indeed that no longer exist. A pragmatist does not judge music itself to be either good or bad. Its worth lies totally in its ability to bring the results assigned to it. The motto of the pragmatic music director is, "I'll do anything to get the message across."

However, as a foundation for music ministry, pragmatism fares no better than aestheticism. In the first place, pragmatism creates a false dichotomy between medium and message, music and gospel, in which each may go its own way without regard for the other. Such a separation of means and ends effectively destroys the more useful premise that, for gospel witness, ends ought to determine means. How one communicates should be dictated by what one communicates—the music and the message must be organically related. The pragmatist is unconcerned that the two may be in conflict and so uses music uncritically as a message lubricator, sweetener, or psychological conditioner. Whatever music will make the acceptance of the message easier, more palatable, and as reflexive as possible is adopted—even if it conflicts with the message itself. The pragmatist, in the name of communication, emasculates the gospel by using commercialized music to sell it. The gospel is stripped of its full integrity and power, and manipulative marketing techniques supplant the work of the Spirit.

Second, pragmatism does away with objective standards. One cannot talk about a "good" or "bad" composition as a piece of music. Its worth is thought of in terms of the results it brings. Seen from the extreme subjective standpoint, music has no accountability for value, no standards save acceptability, and no quality control except results. It loses its inherent worth and its freedom to speak. Forcing the medium to give up its musical integrity is to make it a prostitute. It cannot be considered a true art form at all. Pragmatism is based upon a relativistic worldview in which standards, authority, and prophetic purpose do not exist in any meaningful way.

Third, pragmatism is illogical. It does not hold together philosophically. Elton Trueblood, noting that pragmatism's insidious influence has extended beyond scholarship into everyday life, says:

> The crucial fallacy of pragmatism is the falsity of its own inner contradiction. It appears to uphold the idea that all truth is relative, but relative to what? Since it cannot say "relative to objective truth," it is forced to make pragmatism itself its center of reference. A brilliant critic of pragmatism in history has pointed this out in the following passage: "Professor Commanger's plea is a plea that we should conform to something, i.e. the pragmatic idea. He refers to what he calls 'the first lesson of pragmatism: damn the absolute!' but at the same time he is himself pleading that we should receive the pragmatic ideal as if it were an absolute. The philosophy that damns the absolute is strangely revealed as the absolute philosophy." To make a new absolute out of the doctrine that there is no absolute is obvious confusion.[8]

Thus the pragmatic base so popular with church musicians is found wanting. It dilutes the gospel by allowing the music to be separate from and unaffected by biblical discipline; it naively supports a worldview in which the absence of objective musical standards often accompanies the erosion of biblical authority; and it is found wanting philosophically because of its own internal inconsistencies.

Aestheticism and pragmatism, though, are seldom carried through in a complete and systematic way. Pragmatism may take from the aesthetic a remote and contorted regard for musical quality; aestheticism often draws from the pragmatic a reluctant and disdainful recognition of the necessity of being practical and success-oriented in a very "unidealistic" world.

However, shifting values and standards produce a philosophical unrest that keeps a ministry of music from being all it could and should be. As already noted, without a coherent, comprehensive, and creative basic philosophy, a church music program is like a rudderless ship driven about by a shifting wind. Ministry founders.

Biblical Counterpoint

We have established the inescapability of having a philosophy, the need for a credible working philosophy of music, and the necessity of rejecting aestheticism and pragmatism. That leaves us with the question: What is a better basis for church music ministry?

It would seem that a profitable line of inquiry concerning music in the church would be to develop a foundation based on the church's distinctive—an allegiance to truth as revealed in Holy Scripture. Erik Routley has shown that biblical truth is of paramount importance in addressing the problems of music in the church.[9] Biblical truth speaks to all situations.

If theology is to be the foundation of our value system, then clearly the musician's regard for musical art cannot be allowed to become idolatrous. By the same token, methods will not be worshiped; rather, they will be determined by theological presuppositions. Music directors will not bow at the shrine of success. There will be no conflict between artistry, spirituality, and methodology.

In the theological realm, the finite mind can best understand truth within the tension of apparent opposites. God cannot be contained by one-sided propositional statements. As soon as we think we have discovered all revealed truth, we discover something else that may seem contradictory but actually widens our previous understanding. Jesus was fully human yet fully God. God is immanent yet transcendent, sovereign yet permissive. Our finite minds understand God in dynamic paradoxes—in musical terms, a counterpoint.

Methodologically, it is imperative to note the creative tension apparent in the discovery of biblical truth, for precisely this type of tension is at the heart of a dynamic and creative church music ministry. In our quest for a workable philosophy we will discover many seeming contradictions, each standing alone in its rightness but showing fuller truth in relationship to the others—a beautiful contrapuntal design that forms the philosophical basis of a pastoral music ministry.

2 | *The Doctrine of Creation*

We begin with the doctrine of creation because of its fundamental importance to both theology and art. From a theological standpoint, Langdon Gilkey notes that God's creatorship is "the indispensable foundation on which the other beliefs of the Christian faith are based."[1] The doctrine also supports the artistic enterprise. God as creator has given creative gifts to humanity: the artistic raw material of our world, personal creative ability, and the compulsion to create in freedom.

Creation, Dependence, and Independence

The Bible begins: "In the beginning God created . . ." (Gen 1:1 KJV). Here we are told that God exists and is Creator. Subsequent verses detail God's creative acts in the making of the world. Nothing is said about his being loving or just or holy. The first mention of God simply substantiates the Almighty's presence and his being a creator. God's creating is not fortuitous nor is it unrelated to the divine character. Rather, the process of creation reveals something of God's very nature: he is the Creative One. Appropriately, the historic confessions of the church (such as the Nicene Creed and the Apostles' Creed) state at the outset their belief in God as maker: "We believe in one God, the Father, the Almighty, maker of heaven and earth," and again, "I believe in God, the Father Almighty, maker of heaven and earth." This doctrine's priority for the church's theology is also an indication of its fundamental importance for the church's music.

To begin, God creates *ex nihilo,* out of nothing. God imagines the unimaginable and creates the uncreatable. He originates primal elements and rearranges those previously created. God is under no compulsion to create but does so freely and willingly. The Almighty's making is supernatural and purposeful, ultimately unique. The Creator is entirely separate from what is created, and his creation exists only as he sustains it.

Humans, on the other hand, cannot create *ex nihilo* and therefore rely upon God and the created order. For example, whatever artists make is dependent upon preexistent material—be it sound, color, or stone; the artist merely reorganizes these God-given elements into some meaningful reality.

> In the truest sense artists do not "create," they can only represent, symbolize, or translate what is given. At best they can take materials such as pigment, stone, words, or musical symbols, and rearrange them in such a way as to give communicable impressions of their ideas.[2]

Although some hold that the artist is an autonomous maker, artistic creation is undeniably bound to the physical matter that God has created. Life itself is dependent on God the Creator and Sustainer. All people, even composers, performers, and listeners, are absolutely and utterly dependent.

On the other hand, a certain independence is needed to create works of art. Individuals, freely created by God, are given a like freedom by the Creator. Thus they have free will and are responsible for their own free activity. For example, freedom in personal decision making is the basis of human personality and involves "adding qualities and dimensions to personality that simply were not there, and would not be there now, apart from the free act."[3] There is a sense that something new, fresh, and unique is emerging. So it is in the making of artistic works. Freedom is necessary. The artist's autonomous decisions in composing a piece of music bring into being that which has not existed. Thus while people cannot create in the primal sense, they can create works that are *sui generis,* completely original. In this limited sense we can assert that artists are independent of their Maker and create uniquely.

Human making is thus dependent on preexistent stuff, yet the decisions required by the creative act show the need for independence. We must rely both on God and on ourselves. We are dependent yet independent. Consequently, church musicians, as artists, need to acknowledge their dependence and create in humility. All music making is a gift of a loving God. Musicians should not treat this gift haughtily or lightly, but reverently and seriously.

Musicians are also independent. They possess a certain sense of creaturely exaltedness and sovereignty. Their autonomy is shown by the independent choices they make. Such autocratic decisions are the basis of human creativity and are at the heart of the creative process. Consequently independence is necessary in the creating and recreating of music. Godly music, the vehicle and medium through which the church musician accomplishes the pastoral call, is very much a product of the free act. Artists make their own decisions. They are self-sufficient.

The church artist, more than any other person, needs to realize the implications of such a contrapuntal stance. The church musician, being independent yet dependent, relying on self yet on God, and creating in freedom yet being bound, is caught in the tension between humility and exaltedness. The balance achieved in the creative application of these opposites will give a proper perspective to the music ministry. On the one hand there will be utter reliance on the Almighty and a tendency for self-deprecation; on the other hand there will be personal initiative and, in the right sense, pride in fulfilling individual capabilities. Church musicians must exist in a "humble exaltedness." Without abasement or arrogance they are called to be open channels of creativity—the result of a cooperative venture between the Creator God and the creator musician.

The Natural World and Form

The doctrine of creation affirms the basic goodness of the natural world. Nothing in God's created order is intrinsically evil. This conclusion does not mean that the world is perfect; it too is inextricably involved in the fall and needs to be redeemed. Nevertheless, nature is a gift from God, has potential, and is fundamentally good.[4] Consequently the artist must respect it.

The doctrine also suggests that creation was purposeful. That is, in imposing form upon primal chaos and order upon confusion, God manifested purpose, the process of form-giving being an intrinsically purposive action. Moreover, God's motivation was exclusively love, divine love, carried out within the context of divine freedom. Thus, to say "God creates" is to say that in freedom God lovingly gives form to purpose.

This orderliness, or form, woven into the fabric of the universe, is a requirement for artistic intelligibility. Underlying creation is design, not chaos. Music, as part of the created order of our world, must adhere to the precepts of natural creative process if it is to be worthy. Artistic musical form shows forth the orderliness and purposefulness of God's creation. Without coherence, shape, purpose, or form, good music is not possible.

Much contemporary philosophical thought scorns the idea of order in our world. Themes such as "Existence is meaningless" and "Life is absurd" are not uncommon. In an art such as music, which lacks the definitive symbols of language, the same philosophy of meaninglessness, absurdity, and purposelessness can be communicated through lack of form. For example, believing that "Simple minds cling to the illusion of an orderly, purposeful universe because it gives them a sense of security,"[5] John Cage musically expresses the philosophy of the absurdity of meaning in life through an aleatory (chance) process of musical composition. There is no coherence, shape, meaning, or form to it. Musically he portrays the world and all therein as accidental, purposeless, and chaotic—the product of chance.

However, an allegiance to the biblical doctrine of creation—which holds that God imposed form upon formlessness, that the world has purpose and meaning (which is to say it has form and possesses a goal toward which it is moving), and that the natural world is basically good—demands that the creative artist's work mirror reality. People crave wholeness, and art and religion both deal with reality in a holistic manner. Without the universal artistic ingredient of form, music ceases to be art because it has no goal or purpose. In reflecting the philosophy of purposelessness, aleatory music is absolutely useless for any kind of affirmation concerning God's world and is therefore worthless as church music. It is incumbent upon musicians to be aware of the artistic qualities that give music its coherence and shape. Music that is well crafted affirms this aspect of the doctrine of creation; music that is chaotic because it lacks coherent form denies the doctrine.

Creatio Continua and the Church

The doctrine of creation is concerned not only with the original purposeful bringing into being of matter out of nothing, *creatio ex nihilo*, but also with God's care and sustenance of the world, *creatio continua*. The world itself and everything in it is continuously supported by the ongoing process of creation. This doctrine contends that the work of creation is never finished, unlike the view that God created a world which, like the watchmaker's watch after having been wound, is self-reliant and functions independently of its Maker. *Creatio continua* holds that the maintenance of our world is the continuance of creation and cannot be separated from it.

> To say that he has created involves saying that he is creating now. To sustain is to continue to create, not merely to maintain that which has been created.[6]

Ongoing creation, then, is very much a part of our existence. Without God, the world would cease to exist. But with an immanent God, the world is continually shaped and moved toward the destiny the divine has chosen for it.

Creatio continua is partially our responsibility. God ordered that humans be appointed agents of his continuing creative activity. In the opening chapters of Genesis, human responsibility (referred to as "having dominion over the earth") is, in fact, a prominent theme.[7] The duty of exercising dominion is central to human existence, for it is woven into the very fabric of living. This responsibility to "subdue" the earth and to have dominion over it has been called by theologians the creation mandate. It is a divine charge to all people to live out their creaturely existence creatively and fully.

The mandate to fulfill the potential of this world through human creativity is an important responsibility. But the task is not greater than the God-given ability for accomplishment. People are by nature imaginers and inventors, though in their fallen state they need to be reminded again and again that they do not automatically live creatively. Effort is required. They need a far-sighted vision of what the world might become and the will to implement that vision. In thus fulfilling the creation mandate, we become an arm of God's *creatio continua*, his continuing creation.

Humans were given not only a mandate for the general care and development of the world, but a cultural mandate as well.

> Implicit in the doctrine of creation, then, is its cultural mandate and the call to a creative integration of faith with learning and culture. It is a call . . . to explore the wisdom of God in every area of thought and life, and to replenish the earth with the creativity of human art and science.[8]

Emil Brunner illuminates this point of human responsibility for cultural development when he says:

> The capacity for culture and the desire for culture are characteristic marks of the Divine creation of humanity. Hence culture [art, education, science, etc.] is both God's gift and man's appointed duty; it is a gift, in so far as man cannot help creating culture, and it is a duty, in so far as apart from it he has no right to exist, because otherwise he does not realize his God-given purpose in creation.[9]

We are not merely to accept uncritically the cultural environment in which we live, but are to take action in making it what it could and should be. To form the world culturally is part of human responsibility.

The cultural mandate is one of the most important, though elusive, tasks faced by the Christian artist. The temptation to withdraw from the world because of the steady march of culture away from theistic values is certainly always there. But the stronger temptation is an uncritical adoption of declining cultural values. Reducing art to the commercial level, to aesthetic insignificance, to sheer entertainment (religious or not) is to misuse, even profane, the creative gift. It is not a worthy pursuit. Artists are prophets, and Christians in the arts should take seriously the influence they have in shaping the values and vision of culture. They are to take the stuff of creation and incarnate it into a meaningful form that speaks deeply and powerfully of the fundamental but often invisible truths of our existence: birth, life, death, tension, release, relationship, tragedy, ecstasy, newness, eternity, suffering, sound, silence, redemption, and so on. The cultural mandate is a call to forsake that which is trivial and embrace that which is worthy.

Culture is what people make it. It is not innately antithetical to religion nor can it be assumed to be automatically hospitable to religion. Culture is simply the mode of living here and now in the world of the fall. It reflects the worldview emphases that are prevalent in the everyday life of the general population. Although part of culture, the Christian faith in its pristine form transcends culture, imparting to it a supernatural message that should be proclaimed with a certain tender, loving concern for the cultural realm. The church needs musicians with the gumption to adopt and stick to musical standards that are theistically based, recognizing that the culture's traits that will be evident in its dominant music (currently pop music of various styles and types) may not be biblically grounded. Today extreme relativism, hedonism, pluralism, materialism, and amoralism are the prime characteristics of the dominant western worldview. They are incongruent with Christianity. Consequently church musicians should not legitimize and propagate such values by using music based on those values. Attention to cultural standards is well within the scope of the church's active concern.

The church music director must see to it that the church takes seriously its part in fulfilling the creation and cultural mandates in our world. There actually is no choice if ministry is to be all that it should be, for "Art creates culture; it creates values and meanings by which a society fulfills its destiny. . . ."[10] The church musician cannot afford to sit idly by, leaving the formation and direction of culture to the unregenerate. The doctrine of creation, if it is to be believed and acted upon, puts the church in the forefront of artistic activity. Taking the cultural directive seriously would revolutionize church music. The church body as a whole would welcome great art rather than resist it. Though the high artistic standards of the best musicians appear to be less and less acceptable to many Christians, music directors must fulfill their prophetic role by using great art to help people see and hear far more than they are comfortable with. The visionary integrity of the individual artist and the visionary integrity of an individual church music program could do much to encourage the wider church to live out its corporate life creatively and with artistic integrity. Enthusiasm for such prophetic music ministry would change the artistic climate of the church from an often inflexible conventionality to a flexible originality. The cultural mandate to explore, develop, and create would become a way of life. The church would literally become a community of creators.

The cultural mandate, coming from the broader and more general creation mandate, also has a sense of continuing creation. Cultural development cannot be cut off from *creatio continua*, for it is just as real in the cultural realm as in the natural realm: God continues to create by preserving, utilizing, and developing what he has created through human co-creators.

Cultural *creatio continua* speaks to the necessity of remembering and understanding the past as a guide for ongoing creation. We cannot let history go unnoticed or uninterpreted and still have wisdom for creating the new. In contrast to the Greek cyclical views, Christianity maintains that there is historical progress in the world. The Hebrew-Christian worldview affirms that God reveals himself to us in terms of real events in time. In Acts 10 and 13, Peter and Paul do not give metaphysical discourses but recite the story (i.e., historical events). The Christian religion is a faith primarily grounded in past events, and the continuation of that faith is a matter of remembering and interpreting those events. "In short, He [God] is the *Lord of history*, working through men and nations whom He has raised up to fulfill His purpose."[11]

Hence, the church has a definite mission under the cultural mandate to preserve its cultural heritage for the present and the future. It must promote a positive stance toward the immense store of fine artistic works as we gratefully use them as the basis for the ongoing process of cultural creation. We should regard history neither as a limit beyond which we cannot go nor as a nonessential which we may disregard.

> The man who would live only out of the "now" is surely as immature as he who would regress into the past; and after all, amnesia is a worse sickness than nostalgia. Man does not live by the present alone, neither does he live by the future alone, and to reject tradition is simply to dismember the self. As memory is necessary to the sanity of personality, so tradition sustains the collective personality of a people.[12]

Music has a vital function in the church's preservation of its heritage and that of the broader culture. As we have stated, a primary task of Christianity is to make known its past, and music can be a means to that end. The church music program must neither stifle nor neglect music that belongs to another age. Again, the cultural mandate makes it imperative that the church preserve the past because of its responsibility to the wider culture and because of the historical nature of the church itself. The links and ties to the past, the communion of saints, and the realization that the Christian church has a historical heritage that nourishes the present are important reasons for using great music of the past in the church service.

We must avoid an "either/or" situation relative to old and new music.

> Exclusive commitment to a liturgical-musical past imprisons the church in its past history. Exclusive commitment to an often vapid present imprisons the church in a rootless now.[13]

Cultural *creatio continua* is a matter of treating the past, present, and future as a unit. A music program should be balanced and integrated in all of its creative activity.

Historical *creatio continua* also speaks to the artist as a creator. In the finest sense of the term, the artist is a traditionalist. That is, the artist builds upon inherited artistic practice as new possibilities are explored. T. S. Eliot wrote:

> [Tradition involves] in the first place, the historical sense, . . . and the historical sense involves a perception, not only of the pastness of the past, but of its presence; the historical sense compels a man to write not merely with his own generation in his bones, but with a feeling that the whole of the literature of Europe from Homer and within it the whole

of the literature of his own country has a simultaneous existence and composes a simultaneous order. This historical sense of the timeless as well as of the temporal and of the timeless and of the temporal together, is what makes a writer (or an artist in any field) traditional.[14]

So tradition forms a base of operations, the place from which new horizons expand. Knowledgeable composers work with one face toward the past and one toward the future, influenced by history and by the developing art of the present. If composers get too far from tradition in their contemporary musical development, their music is likely to have mostly shock value. Historically, it is difficult to find a single composer whose music became significant and revered, who ignored the past by not building upon accepted musical practice. It is implicit in creation that one cannot profitably discard tradition. God does not intend his people to ignore the past but rather to build upon it as the evolutionary process of culture, *creatio continua,* goes on.

Creativity

At this point in our discussion, people can be said to create as a result of the responsibility cast upon them in the creation mandate. Formed by God, everyone is given the task of responding to God's call to be a co-creator. We are to be creative as God is creative. The musician employed by a church is not exempt from this call. There is a mission to fulfill under the cultural mandate. We shall further develop this when we deal with the *imago Dei*, but for now, suffice it to say that as an artist the music director must design the parish music program to encourage the full development and use of the best creative gifts people have. In response to the Creator's call, the music director needs to enlist the entire church body in fleshing out the creative potential given it by God.

"Creative," "creating," and "creativity" are words often nebulously used in conjunction with some vague idea of the new or the novel. They are usually used without regard to qualitative considerations. The loose usage of these terms makes it difficult to be precise in talking about such a topic as "creation." Thus, a definition is in order. Our use of the words "creative," "creating," and "creativity" will be technical. They will refer to *that which breaks new ground imaginatively and with integrity.* To be "creative," then, means to originate with artistic excellence.

Such a definition is derived from looking at God's creation as a model. His imagination is boundless, and that which he creates is not shoddily or poorly made. True, we cannot create as God creates, and our activity cannot be directly analogous to his, but we can see in God's creation an example and a directive that people are to create with purpose, meaning, and a sense of imaginative individuality. The beauty of nature gives us a clue as to the direction creativity should take. Wherever we look, from the full breadth of the landscape down to the microscopic cell, we see beauty and order without exact duplication of anything. Our own creation will be but a shadow of this heavenly creation, but it absolutely must be at least a shadow. Whenever human beings become selfish, petty, lazy, indifferent, small, or unconcerned in their creating, that creative activity will be far from being what God intended.

The essence of musical creativity is giving worthy form to new ideas: imagination wrapped in integrity. What has not been done before is the composer's domain. "Music which sounds old-fashioned when it is new is almost always valueless because it is bound to be derivative."[15] By this, Gordon Jacob means that the work is essentially a copy, lacking in creativity. Imagination is the essential ingredient that distinguishes fancy from idea, making from craftsmanship. Imagination fares best when it is disciplined and cultivated, and it is helpless in pure fantasy, needing the direction of the intellect. Good, imaginative musical ideas are capable of artistic development, and good, imaginative craftsmanship develops those ideas so that imaginative newness is clearly and profoundly articulated. Samuel Coleridge saw imagination as a force analogous to God's original creation in the forming of new realities. If we interpret the word "analogous" to mean "similar in principle but not the same as," we can agree. Imagination is the womb in which the creative seed is conceived and developed. It is the lifeblood of all artistic activity; without it there is no art.

Creativity has two general phases, the subjective (that which is intuitive) and the objective (that which is crafted). The first is a matter of the creative unconscious, the idea; the second is a matter of giving good form to or incarnating the idea. Of course both are linked together differently with each artist and in a way which even the artist may not be able to explain. One cannot reduce the matter to a formula. When Renoir was asked about his artistic procedures, he stated that not a single process could be reduced to a formula, including the amount of oil he added to the paint on his palette.[16] One may be able to assimilate technique and skill but still be unable to compose. On the other hand, excellent intuitive artistic ideas alone are no guarantee that worthy composition will result. There is a certain dependence between intuition and the principles of making. They work together. Concerning this process, Archie J. Bahm says:

> One of the sanest, and most astute, evaluations of the various factors involved in creativity, and specifically artistic creativity, is that by Dr. Walter Gotshalk: "In summing up this analysis of artistic creation, we might say that the total creative process embraces a subjective phase and an objective phase, both environmentally nurtured." Furthermore, the subjective and objective phases interdepend, complexly, intricately, dialectically.[17]

The seed of creativity is inspired imagination, which flowers and comes to fruition through the mind.

Church Nurture of Creativity

Both phases of creativity need nurture. Creativity responds to—yes, is often determined by—environmental factors. As part of culture, the church should provide that nurture for its musicians. It ought to be the base of artistic operations for its members. It is here that the regenerate ultimately belong. The church is the Christian musician's cultural home because it is the guardian, proclaimer, and actuator of those biblical principles upon which the art of fine music is founded. The church must not merely tolerate artistic enterprise "out there" but see to it that it nourishes its own.

An understanding of creative nurture is necessary if the church is to live out the cultural mandate. The church, concerned with artistic nurture because of the creation and cultural mandates, should make a strong effort to remove the prevalent causes of artistic inertia within its sphere of activity. As a community of believers, the church must actively contribute to making the environment conducive to fostering the full use of the creative gift. Certain common blocks need to be removed.

Complacency on the part of the church body toward music in general and new music in particular is one of the biggest problems the church musician will face. The uninterested, uncaring attitude of many congregations toward originality is well known. Only when the ceaseless round of the expected is sharply broken is there likely to be concern—and only then to insure a return to the comfortable and the familiar. Seldom does a congregation make creativity the norm. When there is no demand and no support for imaginative newness, a barrier is formed environmentally that keeps all but a venturesome few from developing church music programs worthy of the creative example given by the Creator. To be satisfied with things as they are, to be complacent about newness, is to provide an atmosphere that stifles the creative gift.

Conformity is another hindrance to creativity. In some ways it is easier to deal with than the uncaring attitude of the complacent, because conformity is active. It demands doing even if the doing is following a prescription. Yet creativity is the opposite of conformity by its very definition. Predetermined formulas and clichés render a music that is dull and repetitive. "To say that a creative artist would not incline to repeat himself exactly is an understatement: he is incapable of it."[18] Thus, music composed as a result of forced conformity to the church's dictates in matters of popular taste, harmonic idiom, melodic line, or what have you, is composed with the "artist" in a straitjacket and is bound to evince a shriveled creativity, if not a contorted, contrived, mechanical, and forced one. It is well known that the church has not only accepted such conformity from mediocre artists but has actively demanded it of many who have tried to do better. The result has been a legendary conflict between those artists who (even unknowingly) have taken the creation mandate seriously and the church that purports to stand for truth but in actual practice often denies it. Such a rejection of the practical working out of the creation mandate should cause people to pause and consider their posture in the matter. A desk-bound executive

> cannot dictate to the artist who will illustrate a book what kind of pictures go on which pages. If what he does is to come alive as art, we must give the artist the freedom to develop through the task set before him.[19]

Rather than demand conformity, the church should give opportunity to the artist, who, under the influence of the Spirit, creates as a member of the Christian community. By sponsoring and encouraging the composition, performance, and appreciation of music that breaks new ground imaginatively and with integrity, the church testifies in deed to its God-given task of being a beacon of truth in our world.

In addition to removing the blocks of complacency and conformity regarding the artist's work, the church can also help the artistic enterprise by ministering to the personal needs of the artists. They have their complement of fears, dreams, hopes, pride, failure, inner tensions, conflicting motivations, and so on, which may get in the way of effective creative effort. These personal problems are matters that the church can deal with successfully because the gospel of Jesus Christ provides healing, a loving community, and proper goals. The church can provide an essential part of the personal nurture needed by the artist in ministering reconciliation, love, acceptance, and wholeness. The artist needs the church and the church needs the artist.

The church, then, has an active role to play in the fulfillment of the cultural mandate. That it is sorely needed can be seen by society's denial of the doctrine at every turn. We live in an age when the artistic scene is increasingly dominated by the cheap and facile "creativity" of popular culture. In truth, our society is saturated by the pop syndrome. It is strung out by a hackneyed triviality that is strangling societal appreciation for genuine creativity. The church's mandate to be an agent of creative endeavor has suffered tremendously. The biblical injunction to be creative is at risk.

Summary: Creative Worth and a Church Imperative

We have noted that creation is a matter of forming from the unformed, even as God created order from chaos; the natural world is essentially good; God creates not out of compulsion but in freedom; people have been given the responsibility and the freedom to create culture; there is an orderly process in creation that is evolutionary rather than revolutionary; the composer is caught in the balance between dependence on God and dependence on self in the subjective intuitive idea stage of creation and in the objective form-giving phase; God is glorified both in nature and through human endeavor; creativity needs nurture; and, the essence of creativity is imaginative newness in integrity. Each of these must be acknowledged and acted upon by the church. Whenever composers create or the church utilizes something that is trite, banal, unimaginative, or undisciplined, they have denied the doctrine of creation. God's intent is that earthly creativity reflect heavenly creativity.

The church ignores these principles from the doctrine of creation at its own peril. We have been commanded to be creators, and when creativity stagnates we become less than God intended. To be God means to be creative; likewise, to be human means to be creative. In bringing both together, the church must firmly and unequivocally establish that Christians are to live out the doctrine of creation in all of its glorious fullness and splendor.

Through the arts we share in God's ongoing work and celebrate the goodness of his work. We are on a pilgrimage—always moving, wrestling, creating. The church and its musicians must willingly endure the travail of birthing worthy art. The biblical injunction to

> sing a New Song before the Lord, means that it must be new . . . . This requires the ultimate in creativity and therefore the deepest involvement of the most creative elements in our midst.[20]

We are being ever called, even in our day, to "sing the praise of God freshly."[21]

We make a fatal mistake, however, in assuming that the church needs new music without qualification. Newness is no guarantee of worth. For example, pop is ever new (the Top 40 hits change regularly) but characteristically its essence is far less creative than that of the greatest art. Worthy creative endeavor eschews the impermanence of the banal and the trite. To say that music is new is not enough; it must have compositional integrity, creative spark, and craftsmanship. Furthermore, it must proceed along a logical evolutionary path. If we believe that God is a painstaking craftsman in all his works, then

> it behooves us as His children to be forever dissatisfied with anything but the best quality that we can produce or encourage our neighbor to produce. If men have been set by God upon the earth to "subdue" and "have dominion over" it, this is also a mandate to learn how to command the best use of all the forms of art.[22]

Knowing that the culture in which we live violates God's intention by pressuring men and women into emasculating their God-given abilities as makers and appreciators of art, the church music program needs to take active steps to widen and deepen the church's scope of influence in the artistic realm.

The urgent necessity of fully implementing the biblical idea of creativity is apparent when we analyze the quality of our church music. Much of it falls far short of showing the kind of newness, inventiveness, and integrity consistent with the biblical standard. Many church musicians feel compelled to assume creative standards commensurate with popular culture rather than adopt the biblical pattern of imaginative ongoing creativity. A decline in mainline church attendance, the preoccupation of some evangelicals with numerical success, and an emphasis upon unprincipled evangelism, a goodly portion of which has been based on the business/consumer model; the diminution or dissolution of music education programs in grades K–12, whether in public, parochial, Christian, or home-school systems; the rock revolution of the fifties and sixties with its subsequent stylistic spin-offs; and especially the large-scale cultural swing away from the traditional values of the Judeo-Christian worldview have all combined to lower the creative norms of church music composition.

It is particularly important to note this trend because much inferior music being written and disseminated to churches is labeled "new," as if that were the prime criterion for using it. "New" means nothing if it is not creative (i.e., breaking new ground imaginatively and with integrity). Much of the religious "new" is a commercialized variety of afterthought, a warmed-over version of pop music's last frontier, the wake of everchanging fads, a copy of its nonchurch counterpart. A considerable amount of contemporary religious composition (including much "Contemporary Christian Music") has not the slightest relationship to biblical creativity. Let the church take heed!

Inevitably the question arises: Who is to say that a particular piece of music is creative? If one accepts the naturalistic assumptions that standards are a matter of taste and that one taste is as valid as another (so that there is no "good" or "bad"), then that is the end of it. Carried to its logical conclusion, this assumption implies that all music (and everything else for that matter) is of equal value. But such a stance is erroneous and intolerable for Christians. It implies that instead of being fallen everyone is perfect, that God has given all people similar gifts, which they all use equally well, and that the world is devoid of any consistent and coherent value system. Lead then becomes as valuable as gold; any ointment would have served for Mary's anointing the feet of Jesus; any tribe, trained and ordained or not, could have provided temple music. The biblical writers could not have commented on the beauty of a flower, the beauty of the body, or the beauty of holiness, for "beauty" and "ugliness" would be synonymous and thus meaningless. Such a philosophy belongs to the absurdists who deny value and authority. It is not a viable option for the Christian.

The search for creativity in a piece of music is the domain of those who have an intuitive *and* knowledgeable grasp of the inner essence of music and musical grammar. But it does not follow that intuition and knowledge will alone produce the best choice. Just as humans know right from wrong, yet often choose to do the wrong, so musicians may know what compositions exhibit the highest creativity yet still choose pieces that are absolutely poverty-stricken from the creative standpoint.

The will is involved. It is a matter of choosing rightly. First, we must know what is best; second, we must have the conviction that we ought use the best because using the best is a norm of God's economy. Scripture does not support the idea that either bad, good, better, best are of equal value or that our choice of them should generally be from the poorer categories. God's will is for us to choose the highest and the best as he defines or models it. This is true from matters of salvation (read the Gospels) to matters of personal hygiene (read the Pentateuch). The director's having a Ph.D. in music is no guarantee that the music program will be a paragon of creative virtue!

Music ministers must be able not only to ascertain the creative worth of a piece of music and have the determination to use it, but also to explain these decisions to the community of faith. Teaching the congregation on matters relating to the doctrine of creation as it affects the music used in worship is very much part of the work of ministry. Directors need the ability to reach and use right conclusions. They should also have the ability to make clear to the congregation the reasons for their choices.

Generally, church musicians are in fact able to assess the creative worth of particular musics. Even those who are seemingly happy with a consistent diet of creatively poor music may give themselves away in unguarded moments by such vernacular expressions as "We do some 'good' things" or "We are aiming at the 'classics.' " Granted, musicians will never agree on whether Bach is greater than Beethoven, for example; but there should never be any doubt that J. S. Bach's music has greater musical worth and shows more creativity than that of Ballington Booth, composer and author of the hymn "The Cross Is Not Greater." Christians who have really grasped the doctrine of creation will strive unceasingly to leave behind all that is mediocre and poorly crafted, reaching out instead for creative maturity. We need a renaissance in the careful choice of music of integrity and high creativity in our time—not because of the music, but because the music represents the creatorship of God Almighty and shows our obedience in the matter.

The Christian musician needs to realize the imperative of heeding the biblical command to be truly creative. This is not a trifling matter that can be dispensed with if one feels like it; nor is it an option to be dropped in favor of something else. There is no choice. To live up to God's intent requires that we take seriously his call to live out life creatively. We cannot turn our backs on the full implication of what this means either as composers, performers, or listeners.

Quite frankly, if a knowledgeable observer were asked to name the institution in our society that clearly utilizes the highest musical creativity, we can be sure it would not be the contemporary church. This circumstance is an indictment of how clergy, congregations, and musicians feel about the mandate instituted by God for utilizing the creative potential. Too often all kinds of compositional mediocrity are welcomed into the church while only token recognition is given to music that is solidly crafted upon a sound musical foundation. Creativity is not embraced as a way of life. It is not natural. It is not seen as having much to do with biblical living. Yet it is there in principle—in the Word. This point cannot be stressed enough. The church is a body that maintains that truth is found in the revealed Word of God. If his body, the church, does not practice what it purports to believe, what kind of credibility does it have? It is incumbent upon those who believe that the Bible expresses God's intention to live up to those intentions. God the Creator did not make people to be artistically insensitive or indolent. He gave us a job to do—to subdue (or develop the potential of) a world that, though far from perfect, is still his creation. We cannot in any way escape this mandate. It is ours. The question is: What are we going to do with it?

The church fulfills the creative and cultural mandates as it becomes a microcosm of true creativity. Church music, as an expression of the church's life, should be a vital force in affirming that the church stands for integrity, wholeness, and creativity. The doctrine of creation as exhibited in great church music can show people how to live bountifully amidst the wealth of inspired idea and well-made form. The church must testify to the world, through nurture, use, and attitude, that creativity is both a responsibility and a gift from God the Father, Maker of heaven and earth.

3   *The Imago Dei*

The doctrine of the *imago Dei* is closely tied to that of creation, and we must consider it here in order to gain a fuller understanding of human creativity as it relates to artistic activity, both outside of and especially within the church. Historically speaking, theologians have had numerous differences of opinion in formulating the doctrine's content, so it comes to us in the form of a multitudinous array of statements and counterstatements. For our purposes, an investigation of two components of the doctrine will illuminate and heighten important considerations for a pastoral ministry of music.

Some of the more common interpretations of the doctrine are: God made human beings in his bodily image; the *imago Dei* is centered on personhood; the capacity for knowing moral right and wrong is the *imago Dei*; people exhibit the image of God as they enter into right relationship with God through Jesus Christ; the *imago* is to be found in God-given freedom and responsibility; reason constitutes the image; the image consists in humankind's dominion over the world; and so forth. All of these views undoubtedly have some validity, though our perusal of the doctrine will take us far afield from most of these analyses to a somewhat less familiar, yet fertile, ground.

The last idea mentioned above, dominion, needs special explanation. In the previous chapter we noted that the creation mandate is a God-given obligation to develop the potential of the world by subduing it or exercising dominion over it, even in terms of culture in general and art in particular. Some theologians have believed that the *imago Dei* is to be found here, in the creation mandate, but I think this identification is confusing. The creation mandate can only be accomplished because of our being made in the image of God; but they are not the same thing. Several authors have made this observation. One notes that "this dominion over the animals [the creation mandate] is not in itself the *imago Dei*, but is the first opportunity for the image to be exercised in a definite way."[1] Another says that the dominion of the earth "should not be equated with the fact that he has been created in the image of God—although this mistake is often made—but it should be conceived as its consequence."[2] The *imago Dei* is concerned with the inner nature, the creation mandate with a command for continuing creation. Fulfillment of the mandate may be accomplished because we are equipped to do so through God's gift of the *imago Dei*. The former comes through the latter.

The Broad Imago Dei

The doctrine of the *imago Dei* may be divided into two main parts. The first is a broad interpretation of the doctrine that affects everyone; the second, a more narrow view that applies only to those who are redeemed. Though some theologians prefer one or the other, most agree that both are necessary.

The first, the broad aspect of the *imago Dei*, was formulated to emphasize the fact that the human race, made in the image of God, did not completely lose the image in the fall. Adam and Eve did not become devils when they fell into sin. Not that their godly inheritance was retained without blemish, for if we could have observed them in their original perfection, we might begin to understand Calvin's perspective that what remained of the *imago* after the fall is but "horrible deformity." Yet the image, though tarnished and imperfect, is still there. Even after the fall, humans are made in God's image.

Of the many ways in which theologians have described the *imago* within the broad view, one is particularly important for the church musician, namely, creativity. We have noted previously that God by his very nature is Creator, and a telling adjective to describe him is "creative," since his very makeup is to continually create and recreate. It would be inconceivable to have such a God make a being in his own image and not find that creature bodying forth in its very nature that particular quality that brought life into being in the first place—creativity.

> We are told in Genesis 1:26 that the Creator proposes to make man in His own "image and likeness." There has been much speculation about what might be the meaning or content of this likeness. On the basis of the text itself, we may observe that up to this point in the narrative, the reader has been told only one thing about God that would enable him to attach some content to the notion of likeness to God. He has been told of God's activity as the Creator. One might therefore justly conclude that the meaning of the image and likeness—or at least one meaning of it—is that man shall be *like God in his creativity.* Be creative as your Father in heaven is creative.[3]

Dorothy Sayers, noting that the writer of Genesis has written only of God's creative activity up to the statement, "So God created man in His own image, in the image of God created He him" (Gen 1:27 KJV) says:

> But had the author of *Genesis* anything particular in mind when he wrote? It is observable that in the passage leading up to the statement about man, he has given no detailed information about God. Looking at man, he sees in him something essentially divine, but when we turn back to see what he says about the original upon which the "image" of God was molded, we find only the single assertion, "God created." The characteristic common to God and man is apparently that: the desire and the ability to make things.[4]

Classical Christian thinkers such as Augustine, Bonaventure, and Aquinas, regardless of other differences, all agree that one of the ways the *imago* has been bestowed upon the human race is in the gift of creativity. God intended men and women to be innately creative. The creative force is deeply ingrained in human nature; it is at the center of existence.

The creativity given in the *imago Dei* is an endowment given to all of us. Though few aspire to the level of a Bach or a Beethoven, all participate in the creative gift. The notion that creativity is the possession of only a few is repudiated by the broad sense of the *imago Dei*. Every person is to live bountifully, which is to say, creatively. Actually, many of the various ways of explaining the *imago Dei* in the broad sense can be seen in the creative *imago*. To be a creator requires reason, freedom, responsibility, natural rightness, love toward that which is being created, personality, and a predilection for what is beyond oneself. The *imago* is literally the endowment of talents and abilities (tools, as it were) that make creating possible. It is a mark of being human and applies to all, saint or sinner, regenerate or unregenerate.

Everyone, then, has internal creative forces that indicate a special relationship or correspondence to God and that form the basis of creaturely existence. Living creatively is much more than artistic activity. It is living all of life in such a manner that we fulfill the potential of our humanity. In a sense, one's own life can become a work of art as we exercise our gifts responsibly in freedom. The mundane and ordinary things of life both relationally and environmentally can be materials for becoming and making what is not.

Great artists, however, have unique gifts and can show us with particular lucidity the creative meaning of the *imago Dei*. Emmanuel Chapman notes that "in a certain manner art may be said to be the highest natural likeness of the activity of God."[5] Artists make visible in concrete form what others do not readily see. They apprehend relationships where none appear to exist and see potential in the most ordinary and unlikely things. The artist's making is free, unforced, and inherently purposeful. Artists incarnate pure idea into powerful form in such a way that the resulting beauty is apprehensible and corresponds in some degree to everyone's natural, God-given sensitivity to beauty. The artist's work is not purely utilitarian. The reason for creating is not to force upon the art object a servile subjugation; rather, as an expression of human creativity, art's reason for being is in being beautiful and true. The artist wrestles and overcomes the material of the world so that something unique is brought into being. This doing of something new, this ability to be original, to overcome chaos and formlessness, to see and hear where others know only a void, to bring joy through beauty and truth, is the closest the artist can come (within the broad view) to fully realizing the creative image of God.

The fact that we have a creative nature that can soar to great creative heights does not mean that creativity will always take a wholesome direction. Sloth, indifference, selfishness, pride, or any number of similar things can rob or warp creativity so as to produce the trivial, the mediocre, or the grotesque. Because of disobedience, human creativity is fallen. Though creativity remains part of our glorious heritage, the artist must struggle continuously against the heaviness of the world in the birthing of creations that are excellent. The fall has left its mark. People will always be creative to some degree. The problem is to use our creativity fully, as God intended—a creativity that is the glory of its maker because it is worthy of the Maker.

The broad sense of the *imago Dei* is a bequest from a Creator God. It makes us creative. There is a direct correspondence between the Divine and the human here. Both manifest creativity as a basic characteristic. Nevertheless, human creations are not perfect, though their creators have the capacity of approaching perfection as they strive toward that which is true and good. When the creative gift is exercized "creatively" (breaking new ground imaginatively and with integrity), it shows the *imago* with particular clarity.

Church music is affected by the broad *imago Dei* in that the arts are part of human activity before they are a part of the activity of the redeemed. Christians are first called to creativity by virtue of their humanity. All their activities, including those of church music, should be transformed by a sterling use of the broad *imago*. There is much musical activity in churches, not an unexpected phenomenon given our inclination to be creative. Yet in looking at the activity and the product of the activity—one wonders just how true a picture is being painted by the church of our being made in the creative image of God! Every year thousands of pieces of music are published and performed that have more to do with self-indulgence than with creativity. Poor music, wherever it is found, shows explicitly an *imago* that is far less than that implicit in a composer's God-given creative potential. Church music that does not clearly exhibit genuine creativity has no place in church because it dishonors and demeans the *imago Dei*.

A viable church music program cannot be built if this doctrine is ignored. The musician has an extraordinary obligation to show the broad *imago Dei* by the compositional excellence of the music of congregation, choirs, soloists, and instrumentalists. The music program must be a collective proclamation that the Creator God made men and women to be creators after his own image.

The Narrow Imago Dei

The narrow view of the *imago Dei* holds that the image was destroyed in the fall; that, having come into sin, there remains no vestige of our former stature. Only as we are redeemed, coming to God through Jesus Christ, the perfect image, is the *imago* restored. The image cannot be known outside of a saving relationship with God.

This view of the *imago Dei* may be understood in three different, but not mutually exclusive, ways: (1) we *are in* the image of God; (2) we *are becoming* like the image of God; and (3) we *image* God.

First, we are in the image of God as the propitiatory work of Christ is accepted. Through the atonement the debt of sin has been paid and the new Christian stands before God justified, perfect in righteousness. The *imago Dei* on this level, then, is viewed through Jesus Christ. It shows the believer to be made in God's image, complete, and without blemish. This is how God looks at the redeemed.

Second, we are becoming like the image of God, or to put it another way, being conformed to the image of the Son. Here the Christian life is depicted as a process of growing into Christ's likeness. The Christian's sufferings, trials and tribulations, testings of faith, learning to love more fully, grappling with creative expression, and so on, are a necessary polishing and refining of self so that one's character comes to resemble more clearly that of the Creator and Redeemer. The rough edges, the personality flaws, the hidden secrets of the heart, the warring of the "old man," the indulgence of selfishness and pride, the setting up of idols, all must be surrendered and overcome. As believers slowly move toward what God would have them be, they become more and more like Christ, the perfect image. This life pilgrimage is a growth process. The image grows stronger and brighter the closer one comes to the Source. Christians are "becomers," moving toward the perfect *imago*.

The third way of viewing the narrow *imago Dei* is to understand the word "image" more as an active verb than a passive noun. The Christian "images" God. God is disclosed to the world through observable acts. To image God is to shine as a beacon on a hill so that all might see and hear God in us. Berkouwer says:

> This "being like God" can shine forth as a light in the world. It is the light of good works: Let *your* light shine among the people so that they may *observe* your lofty actions and give glory to your heavenly father (Matt 5:16).[6]

The redeemed tell about God through their actions. To "image" is to make visible, to represent God in deed in such a manner that the meaning behind the action is seen. The *imago Dei* is a "summons to action; a challenge to conduct, a guide to behaviour."[7] Christians in the narrow sense of the image are to set forth an imitation of Christ which lives up to that portrayed in Scripture.

The restoration of the narrow *imago* calls us to a level of faith commitment in which obedience and responsibility to the full implications of the Word are paramount. In Christ we belong in community. We are responsible to God not only for ourselves, but also for our neighbor. The attitude that we must care for the world is deeply ingrained in the Christian faith. We become right with God in order to serve both God and others. The narrow image of God is not inwardly static. Rather, it is outwardly dynamic. The image is nothing if it is not an active and discernible representation of God as we serve him with the gifts he has given us.

> But the actual image is found in the *use* of these created qualities in active and dynamic service of God. Thus and only thus can man reflect God, mirror God, be in God's image. The image of God does not consist of qualities in themselves, but in created man's life *in actu*, in action, and in functioning.[8]

Those who are in loving relationship with the Creator represent him through what they do.

The Christian who withdraws and hides from the world cannot image God. A representer needs an audience to whom God is represented. That audience is the world. We cannot image God in a vacuum, sitting back in isolation waiting to go to heaven. As Christians we are to see the world as a grand opportunity for witness, for showing forth the *imago*, for imaging our "being-like-God." We welcome the world rather than withdraw from it so that we can present to it the full meaning of being made in the image of God. The new birth makes us new creatures who are commissioned to glorify our Creator. We fulfill God's intent and purpose to glorify him as we are *in* the image, as we *become* more like the image, and as we *image* the image.

The imaging of the redeemed needs to affect every sphere of life: economic, social, political, domestic, religious, and aesthetic. A Christian's witness through and to all areas of culture gives the best idea of the breadth and depth of exemplary witness. It is not a matter of talking, of verbal barrages, but rather of expressing God's intention through *what we do*, through a *way of life*. Redeemed imaging, pure and simple, is good action consistent with the Word. It shows the very core of what we really are rather than what we say we are. Redeemed imaging is the proof of our confession. It is our witness to all of culture. Nothing is exempt. What we read, the intensity of our study, how we spend our money, the care for our families, where we go, the help we give our neighbors, our consistency in upholding the moral law, the television programs we watch, *and* the music we listen to, are only a few examples of practices through which we image God to the world.

I have asserted that the broad view of the *imago* can best be explained by the all-inclusive use of the term "creativity." By virtue of our humanity, humans have a creative nature. Though the fall has tarnished it, as creatures made in God's image, we must ever strive to rise to new heights of creative activity.

Redemption affects general creativity. In a well-known passage that draws upon various writings of Nicolas Berdyaev, W. Paul Jones says:

> Man is created in the *imago Dei;* this image and likeness is restored to
> him through the redemptive activity of Jesus Christ. Here is the key to
> the Christian understanding: The God in whose image man has been
> formed and to which he has been restored is the creator God. Therefore,
> redeemed life, life in the Spirit, *is* the life of creativity. Redemption in
> itself is negative; it means liberation *from.* Consequently, the intent of
> redemption, its positive corollary, is liberation *for* creativity.[9]

One must see, then, in the narrow view of the *imago Dei*, an
intensification of our general creative potential because there
is now a direct link through Jesus Christ to the source of all
creativity.

More specifically, we should expect artistic creativity to be
heightened by one's becoming a Christian. Believers are not to
turn their backs on good creative action (breaking new ground
imaginatively and with integrity) though it is unfortunately true
that much so-called "Christian art" is inferior. To the contrary,
Christians need to demonstrate that they are made in the image
of a Creator because they now represent him in a much higher
sense than that of the broad *imago*. The redeemed image God
even through art! Edith Schaeffer comes right to the point
when she says:

> It is true that all men are created in the image of God, but Christians are
> supposed to be *conscious* of that fact, and being conscious of it should
> recognize the importance of living artistically, aesthetically, and crea-
> tively, as creative creatures of the Creator.[10]

And again:

> In other words, are we, who have been made in the image of our Creator,
> and who acknowledge and understand what that means because we
> know God exists, and experience communication with Him—are we to
> be less creative than those who do not know that the Creator made them
> in His image, and who have no contact with Him?[11]

It is easier to ask the question than to actually increase creativity. Yet the arts should be one of the highest manifestations of
the creative gift. Therefore we should expect those made in the
narrow image to reflect God's creativity in greater measure
than do the unregenerate. However, experience has shown that
often Christians make, perform, and appreciate works of "art"

which are so poor that a mockery is made of God-given creativity. A tainted *imago Dei* results.

Redeemed imaging is crucial. It gives credence to the viability of the Christian faith. To show forth God's glory in terms of one's actions is no small matter. It cannot be taken lightly or seen as an option. What a Christian does witnesses, hence the need for choosing wisely and well in the arts.

Summary: Musical Imaging

We have said that in the creation mandate everyone, regenerate or not, is given the responsibility to assist in God's ongoing creation, *creatio continua*. We are endowed with the tools for this task via the broad sense of the *imago Dei,* and create because it is part of our nature. Further, in the narrow sense of the *imago Dei,* Christians face the prospect that through their actions (including their music) *God is made known*. Church music is testimony, and in worship believers use cultural expressions, such as music, to show what God has done, what he means, and who he is.

We noted previously that because of the fall the broad *imago Dei* was weakened. In spite of that fact and in response to the urge to make things, human ingenuity has created great and noble works that glorify the Creator. The narrow view states that the image is a redeemed relationship with God through Jesus Christ. This relationship has the potential to restore God's people to a fuller creativity. The Christian has an active part to play in this restoration as formerly observed when (1) *in* the image, (2) *becoming* like the image, and (3) *imaging* the *imago Dei*.

But one of the scandals of the Christian community is that many Christians feel little compulsion to fulfill the creative potential. What we have said about the need for true creativity in the unregenerate in the broad *imago* must be multiplied for Christians, who participate not only in the broad image but also in the narrow image. The Christian who refuses to rise above vulgarity, mediocrity, and even the good (as opposed to the best) in the arts is exhibiting a distorted, warped, twisted, even mutilated version of the image of God.

If this were not bad enough! The church musician must also contend with the listless discrimination perpetrated upon the general public by many religious periodicals, music publishing firms, music seminars, and Christian radio and television programs. In general, the quality of musical composition is seldom the main focus of attention. It seems that unreasoned bias and blind obeisance are replacing careful evaluation and sound thinking. Conversation about the contemporary church music dilemma "has too often gotten down to the level of a shouting match between the purists who hold that old is good, and the faddists who feel that the latest is the greatest."[12] The cyclical spiral of musical mediocrity is continued by endless publishing of "music that sells," seminars for the general but uninformed Christian music lover held by "prestigious" musicians with commercial musical standards, and the Madison Avenue–style selling of the religious experience of pop music stars with little or no concern for the inherent quality of the music used in the testimony.

Ironically, many of the radio and television programs that purport to witness to the fullness of God's bounteous riches miss the mark when it comes to music. Such riches are supposed to be appropriated in everyday living: spiritually, psychologically, and physically. They are riches set in a sumptuous banquet for all those in the narrow *imago Dei*. And while these radio and television shows often have the very best in the way of equipment, facilities, and staff expertise, the *imago Dei*, the redeemed imaging as it is shown in the general quality of the musical compositions aired from day to day, is often one of emaciated privation, an *imago Dei* gaunt and hollow, a malnourished, spindly, feeble creativity.

These are but a few examples of the religious musical culture that so powerfully confronts the new Christian. The God-given creative potential in the redeemed *imago* is largely cast aside, and a monstrous musical-theological hoax is foisted on the religious world. It is monstrous not only in size and scope but in content. Though feted by commercial entrepreneurs and undiscriminating consumers, music lacking in creative excellence is incongruous with the doctrines of creation and the *imago Dei*. It is distressing that these creators, marketers, and listeners blindly adopt the aesthetic canons of a post-Christian culture. Christians holding a musical value system incompatible with their Christian faith manifest a negative musical witness that hurts the cause of Christ. The resulting malaise, though unintended, is nonetheless devastating.

God the Creator as shown forth by the church musician's music is often a frightening prospect! We image God in the music we make and perform. When the program is hit-or-miss, we show forth a God who lacks purpose and direction; when our work is not well prepared, we image a God who is lazy and slothful; when performance preparation is a last-minute affair, we show forth a procrastinating God; when our performance of music lacks vitality or artistic grace, we portray God as inert; when our musical choices revolve around taste rather than value, God is seen as indulgent and lacking objective standards; and, above all, when the music we choose lacks creativity in the full sense, we image forth a God of "creative" mediocrity. The church musician must take note, for there is no getting around the fact that our actions speak louder than our words.

The question each church musician faces is not, "Shall I image God?" but, "What image will be set forth?" To be created in God's image and then reformed into his image through Christ is to have now an evangelistic reason for setting forth in music a higher and more noble image of God. The human family may be made in God's image in the broad sense, but the Christian specifically images God as Creator and Redeemer in all of his glory. Redeemed imaging is the *imago Dei* at its highest and best. We cannot afford to let it be anything less.

The church musician, then, is responsible for music that sets forth the *imago Dei* to the world. In this way he or she is showing care for others and is fulfilling the Great Commission. This imaging is carried out only when music exhibits a high degree of skill in composition and in performance, for the *imago Dei* is shown through the notes.

4   *The Incarnation*

The incarnation is the main event in God's self-disclosure to the world. Spirit became flesh. Simultaneously Jesus was fully God and fully human, neither nature compromised because of the other. Though human, yet untainted by sin, the Lord's enfleshment was realized through his own free and sovereign will and was motivated by the desire to call us to himself in divine love. His becoming the God-man to mediate between God and a fallen race is indeed the supreme example of that love.

The initiative God took in making a way for people to be reconciled unto himself shows the Eternal united with the temporal, Spirit with matter, the Word in flesh. The incarnation was the divine entering the stream of history in a physical way, thus refuting the notion that while the spiritual is good, the temporal is inherently evil, so that the two are eternally opposed:

> In Christ, the infinite chasm between God and man was permanently traversed. This means no more division between sacred and secular acts. . . . The sacred entered the profane, ending the eternal duality of the Greeks.[1]

Christ's humanity, his being with us in a tangible way, vividly portrays his immanence. God is present in various degrees and levels within creation. The fact that he came in the flesh gives us assurance and comfort that he did not forsake what he created. In Christ, we know and feel that he is with us. He knows our joys, sorrows, failings, weaknesses, and sinfulness, yet he loved us in our fallen condition. He is a God who is here and who cares. Not that Christ became our twin, his divinity superseded by his humanity. Certainly a radical immanence in which the divine is replaced by the human is just as erroneous as a radical transcendence in which God is banished to the heavens, out of touch with the created world and with the day-to-day events of our lives. A balance between immanence and transcendence is needed. And the immanence side of the equation is shown most clearly in the incarnation: God loves so much he has deigned to dwell with us.

Art itself is incarnational. The artist takes the material of the earth and through the creative process causes it to flesh out artistic intent. That which did not previously exist becomes apprehensible. Idea takes upon itself real form; thought is embodied in matter, light, and sound. The "word," as it were, becomes "flesh." Essentially, then, an artist is best seen as an incarnator, one dealing in concrete realities. The church musician participates in the fleshing out process not only through composing but also by performing. That is, music in score form, though having material configuration, really takes shape only when it is actually sung or played. The process of performing, then, is also incarnational.

Four features of the doctrine of the incarnation will concern us here: humility, relevance, form and content, and implicit communication. The doctrine as a whole yields a theological basis for the more pastoral aspects of music ministry. Significantly, the emphases of humility and relevance form a contrasting counterpoint to the previously considered doctrines of creation and *imago Dei*. This juxtaposition is a notable example of paradox that brings a dynamic and flexible approach to ministry.

Pastoral Humility and Love

Humility should be the underlying attitude of the church musician. Such a posture is derived from the example of the incarnate Lord who in becoming human humbled himself. The infinite God became finite man. Richard Crashaw captured a glimmer of this truth when he wrote:

Welcome all wonders in one sight,
Eternity shut in a span,
Summer in winter, day in night,
Heav'n in earth, and God in man!
Great little One! Whose glorious Birth
Lifts earth to heav'n, stoops heav'n to earth.[2]

Christ, stripped of his glory, condescended to become human flesh, emptying himself of his power, place, and authority. He became the lowest of the lowly. He experienced the rejection of adoring and cheering multitudes and was left with only a handful of disheartened and bewildered disciples. He endured humiliation, shame, and bodily and mental suffering, was accused unjustly, and finally died a disgraceful and painful death. Jesus gave up everything to become a servant to those who should rightly have been his subjects. The tenor of the entire Christ-event was humility, as illustrated in capsule form by Jesus' washing the disciples' feet. This act was no mere

> isolated object lesson. It was a drama expressing the total character of Jesus' mission. He stripped Himself of power and privilege. He poured Himself out in the service of mankind. He purged the deepest recesses of the human spirit.[3]

Jesus was indisputably a "man existing for others," as Bonhoeffer puts it. He showed no pretentiousness, no snobbery, no exclusiveness. He kept company with prostitutes and tax collectors as well as with teachers and religious scholars. He turned none away and treated those who came to him with kindness and gentleness. Jesus, the Christ, the Son of God, was a servant.

Christ expects his followers to exhibit a like humility. Using himself as a model he taught the disciples to follow his example:

> Ye call me Master and Lord: and ye say well; for so I am. If I then, your Lord and Master, have washed your feet; ye also ought to wash one another's feet. For I have given you an example, that ye should do as I have done to you. (John 13:13–15 KJV)

Christian leaders are not excused from humble service. They are to endure pain, suffering, and hardship on behalf of those whom they are called to serve. Every Christian (including the church musician) is to emulate the suffering servant image revealed in Old Testament literature and fulfilled in Jesus Christ.

Humility is necessary because in the course of working with the congregation music directors are often called upon (to a greater degree than any other minister) to give up things that are meaningful, even central to their artistic vision. Naturally, music ministers are better trained in music than most parishioners. They have a more refined intuitive artistic sense, broader and deeper knowledge, and greater experience. Musically speaking, they exist on an exalted level; the congregation on a considerably lower one. A musician may therefore be tempted at times to choose music on the basis of a certain musical elitism, believing the congregation's preferences to be beneath consideration. The result is polarization, the musician stubbornly refusing to give up what is assumed to be "correct music" and the congregation not grasping its significance.

It is not that directors necessarily lack good intentions. In an effort to promote good music that communicates the gospel well, musicians work very hard as pastors, conductors, educators, and scholars. The attempt to make the local church music program a model of aesthetic perfection may even become an obsession. But one danger in this is that musical pride, undetected and hidden by good intentions, will fuel the classic breach between the musical standards and desires of the music director and those of the congregation. The musician may perceive the congregation to be uncultured and musically nescient, may resent and consider audacious any suggestion they may have for "updating" the music program. Conversely, the congregation may hold the musician to be an arrogant snob whose air of superiority masks a selfish psychological need to use them for personal musical satisfaction. It is here that the doctrine of the incarnation can bring healing to a painful split—a split that tends to worsen as positions harden on both sides.

The church is a body; it cannot exist without a sense of togetherness between professional staff and people. It is vital that the music director view amateur musical expression through the incarnation. One cannot have congregational togetherness without their full participation and it is unlikely there will be participation if music exists on a consistently higher level than people's ability for comprehension. The Lord, in coming to earth, came to all people. In following Christ's example, it is imperative that musical pride be resisted. The pastoral musician must take into consideration (without condescension) others who are less artistically advanced and those whose musical taste is undeveloped or even aberrant.[4] Only as a church music program begins to take seriously the views of everyone can it be considered incarnational. The minister of music must stoop in humility.

The doctrine of the incarnation demands that musicians become pastors. When the primary concern is for the music itself, the pastoral role, which entails caring for people, will be diminished. Such an emphasis does not do justice to the theology of the incarnation, for it puts the musically immature on a lower plane than those who minister. As a servant, the music director is to wash humanity's feet, to minister to people where they are—not to lament the possibility of having to lower one's station in life.

The incarnational approach to music-making opens up the possibility of serving any congregation, regardless of its present musical standards. The Christian message does not fit in with just a particular cultural situation. Directors must adapt to the customs and expectations of each parish. Initially this may mean lowering one's personal aesthetic standards, or perchance raising them, though this is unlikely. In adjusting to the assembly's level, the director establishes a point of contact with the parish. Pastoral love is demonstrated. The Christian community, as Calvin Seerveld points out, needs leaders who stay close to and form a bond with those who are less proficient in cultural matters. If the church is to fulfill the cultural mandate, its leaders (including the musicians) must not exhibit an intellectualism that will alienate those whom they serve.[5] Concern for music has its place, but in the pastoral ministry of music, concern for people should come first. It is important that we have

competent musicians with a pastoral orientation. Leadership from the aristocratic stance is the result of convictions about musical standards

(and this must be neither despised nor lost); leadership from the pastoral
stance is the result of love, which seeks to enable the people to perform
their liturgy. As in all forms of Christian service, the servant form is the
model.[6]

The church musician, then, shows the humility exhibited
by God in the incarnation by becoming one with the assembly
no matter what its cultural state. The music program's first
concern is for the assembly, rather than a proprietary concern
for the aesthetic worth of music. The pastoral musician's role
is to set aside pride and to minister to people where they are,
a musical enfleshment of the mystery of the incarnation. There
is no time to mourn lack of position, ingratitude for professional abilities, or the unfairness of people who are musically
adolescent but who dictate musical policy. Like all other Christians, musicians need to show God's love as demonstrated in
the incarnation. The philosophical premise and stance of the
music program must be incarnational love. The pastoral duty
of the servant-musician is to care, to be concerned, to show
regard—in a word, to love.

It would be beneficial to pause a moment to reflect on the
word "love." From the foregoing, one might be tempted to
conclude erroneously that pastoral love means no more or less
than doing what people want. Authentic love, though, is much
more than this. It goes beyond what is immediately apparent.
Denying a child the pleasure of consuming an entire box of
chocolate candies does not look like love to the child at the
time. Authentic love does not mean catering to and fulfilling
every fleeting whim of the assembly. It is responsible and takes
into account final well-being.

Communication: Relevance

Every congregation has its own idea about what music is
best suited for worship. The incarnational approach means that
the music director must, without being wishy-washy and weak-
kneed, be responsive to the congregation's thinking, realizing
that church music must be meaningful to them. Their musical
profile must be taken into account. Music which over an
extended period of time is incomprehensible, even baffling,

cannot serve the needs of worship. Music must be intelligible and yet not so obvious and facile as to amount to nothing more than entertainment. Indeed,

> we disobey Him if what we do and sing and say and pray is unintelligible to those who come, or to whom we go. We further disobey this command if we dress up the truths of the Gospel so that they appeal only in a romantic light—so that the death of Jesus gains a "kind of gloss it didn't have." The irrelevance of Christianity, as it appears to many, lies partly in our inability to communicate, and also partly because what we communicate is only part of the truth, or a dressed up version of it.

> Basically the problem is one of communication. . . .[7]

We have discussed the incarnation in the light of the musician's need for a pastoral attitude of humility. Also, we have seen that our concern for people must take precedence over our concern for music. But the doctrine is also highly instructive for communication methodology. On the one hand, we must communicate from a common base of understanding (relevance); and on the other, our communication should say what we intend (content and form). The facts of the communication must not be distorted by the mode of communication.

Both the incarnation and art can be viewed as communication methods. Speaking theologically, we did not go to God. It was God who established the relationship that we could not build ourselves. Human beings bring nothing to the covenant. God accepts us as we are, in sin and degradation. God came to people in terms they could understand. The incarnation is, as it were, a translation of God into meaningful language. The one who dwells in light unapproachable, who is larger than the meanings of human words and symbols, and who as transcendent God cannot be known, comes to us immanently, on our level, in a form that we are able to apprehend. Jesus as created being is then no longer incomprehensible. He becomes unmistakably relevant.

The theme of relevance has been taken up in full force by the contemporary church. Terms such as "identify with," "here and now," "meet the people where they are," "seeker-sensitive," and "all things to all people" (often made into a caricature of

Paul's original intent) are common. The attitude is: "God took on human flesh, now let us not be afraid to incarnate the gospel further into whatever form necessary to get the message across." In our society many believe that cultural forms (such as music) are worldview neutral.[8] Accordingly, any medium, style, or quality is believed suitable for the presentation of the gospel. The key issue is relevance. Since the church has no more important task than communicating the Christian message, some religious leaders feel it is incumbent upon communicators to use those forms that have the widest appeal. Further, some contend that the church needs to abandon the historic nave and chancel, as it were, and move into the street. Shopping malls, entertainment complexes, and drive-ins then become the locations of choice since they are currently considered the most relevant to the average person, especially the "unchurched." Services are packed with music that is stylistically similar to the everyday music listened to by the average attendee so that the church speaks clearly and unmistakably in a language people enjoy. For example, when the music program of a particular church which featured a variety of musics (from "Bach to Rock") alienated the congregation, a survey of their musical tastes was initiated. The result of the survey then became the basis for the music used in "ministry." Since 97 percent of the assembly preferred the music of a middle-of-the-road rock radio station, the church exclusively adopted that style of music for its services.[9] Theirs was a one-sided relevance-driven approach.

Beware! More needs to be said. There is no doubt that the incarnation indicates that communication needs to be relevant. Without relevance there can be no communication. If we assume for the moment that church music is entirely and solely a matter of communication (which it is not), one can see why musical relevance is believed by many to be all-important. But relevance uninformed by the counterpoint of other aspects of the incarnation or salient points from other doctrines, is truth taken to an extreme—a common definition of heresy.

It is instructive to note that Jesus, in taking upon himself human form, remained sinless. He found it possible to be

relevant without participating in the activities of dishonest tax collectors, prostitutes, and thieves. Relevance is important, but it does not mean wholesale assent to a way of life that is diametrically opposed to all that the gospel stands for. It does not mean pretending there are no norms for art; that any artistic "behavior" is acceptable so long as the art form communicates. Surely immorality, for example, may be relevant to our society, but that does not justify it. Moral analogies aside, the following paragraphs present an advantageous way of coming to grips with the problem of relevance and communication as it relates to music in the church.

Knowledge precedes faith. Redemption is predicated upon personal acceptance of the atoning work of Christ. This is literally impossible unless one first knows there is a Jesus whose propitious death and resurrection bring salvation to those who believe. Obviously one cannot believe until one knows what to believe. The only way that this knowledge can be given is through verbal statements. Language—the most effective meaning-symbolization system—is the only way that the facts of the atonement can be given. Church music (speaking of music, not text) cannot challenge language at this point. Explicit meanings are outside the realm of music; music (notes, rhythm, harmony) is unable to give propositional details. Hence music itself need not, indeed cannot, be concerned with the imparting of religious dogma. The direct witness of the gospel is the domain of language—even in a song.

Musical relevance, then, cannot be considered on a par with verbal relevance. Language and music should be understood on two completely different levels. Verbal understanding is specific understanding (as specific as language can get), while musical understanding is less specific. It is possible to answer the question "Do you understand?" regarding a propositional statement, but to answer the same question about a piece of music is to plunge into a tremendously murky area where rational understanding may take many directions. Relevance, insofar as it promotes factual knowledge of the gospel, is far more important to language than to music. Relevance in musical terms is much more akin to general familiarity than to a finely honed understanding. Musical relevance does not have to bear the responsibility for the rational understanding of the literal Word, because that is the domain of language. This is not to say that musical relevance is unimportant. It is important, but it should operate on a less intense plane than is usually assumed.

Relevance, if carried to the extreme, would be the death of a prophetic music program because musical ministry would depend on what is and not what should be. All "oughtness" and compunction for musical rightness would be eliminated. Church music would be driven not by the immutable truth of God's Word but by the vagaries of fads and the fancies of a culture largely out of touch with the divine. The incarnation did show that God stooped to earth. He did lower himself and become human. He did become relevant. *But Christ stooped in order that he might pick us up.* The incarnation can in no way be seen as an excuse for a life of musical deprivation and total cultural determinism. Just the opposite is true. The incarnation is the portal that makes fathomable God's boundless riches of spiritual grace and creative excellence.

Practically speaking, what do we mean when we say church music should be relevant? The prevalent view is that popularity is a precondition for relevance. But Jesus, the incarnate Son, never played to the crowd, yet he was relevant. On the other hand, does anyone believe his relevancy was due to his righteousness and goodness? Actually, he was too good, too holy, too much God to be known readily by us, which is the precise reason for the incarnation in the first place. Being relevant is not a matter either of being well-liked or of being a model of perfection.

Relevance in church music is a matter of being able to identify with the music. That is to say, the music must have something about it that is recognizable and ordinary, both in the configuration of its various musical elements and in its total impact. To begin with, the theoretical musical system should normally correspond to that found within the general culture. One would not impose a strange musical language—say, that of India—on our American church, for our musical system is that of the West. One must also pay attention to the peculiar musical culture of the congregation. This does not mean that the church music program will necessarily contain their favorite music, for such music may be so far from being an analogue of the gospel that its use would be detrimental to the assembly and the cause of Christ (whether they realize it or not). What it does mean is that a congregation's musical culture would be factored into the director's decision-making process. The assembly's capabilities for handling particular musical materials would be part of the mix of considerations necessary for arriving at the best church music for a particular congregation. Obviously an assembly for whom Lawrence Welk or Andrae Crouch is high musical art cannot ordinarily be expected to relate immediately to J. S. Bach or Hugo Distler. Knowing the precise skills and aptitudes of a congregation is very important in this matter of relevance.

We must also deal with the general cultural mindset of the congregation, noting its geographical location, church denomination, social class, average age, and general educational level. Taking into consideration these background facts, the biggest and most intractable problem the music director will face is the absolute intolerance on the part of increasing numbers of Christians for church music that is stylistically unlike the popular music they listen to every day. In years gone by we assumed each church had its particular "brand" of music. This is no longer generally true. Now most religious bodies are beginning to use stylistically similar music; they are accepting features of a worldview that is heavily concerned with pleasuring the self. To be relevant, it is said, means programming what people like and enjoy. This is not a matter of musical aptitude but musical taste. Many people who are well educated, even musically, are so conditioned to see church music as entertainment that they cannot easily see it any other way. Some may relate well to great music outside the church but shut off their musical capacity (often unknowingly) in church. The problem is the hold pop music has on culture—a hold that tends to strangle all other musical expressions, like it or not. No matter how much directors lament this hold, they will never bring people around to a more biblical orientation if they give up, pretend there is no problem, or unite with those who advocate an extreme pop relevance. The director must face this dilemma head-on and use relevance as only one factor in seeking the right music for the assembly.

After coming to know both the congregation's preferential musical level and its potential musical level, a music minister will have a very good beginning for a responsible relevance. A balance between the two will relieve the musician from basing musical choice on mere taste and provide the latitude necessary for a prudent pastoral music ministry—a latitude that will have room for the ordinary and for the sterling.

It may be difficult to know just how far cultural conditions should be allowed to determine the musical forms that make up our worship services. The individual situation will determine, to a greater or lesser degree, the music used. Music appropriate in one context is not necessarily appropriate in another. Even within a single congregation differences in age, taste, and cultural conditioning will affect the choice of music. One needs a certain sense of a conglomerate center from which a balanced, yet directional, approach can be taken. In appraising a congregation's musical tolerance one observes their level of understanding without losing sight of one's prophetic musical goals, which are determined by biblical and theological standards.

God, given his infinite greatness and creativity, could have disclosed Jesus Christ to the human family in any number of different ways. The method chosen clearly indicates God's understanding both of human nature and of Christ's mission. God chose this method because he knew the sum total of our situation: creaturely, fallen yet made in his image, proud, rebellious, and in need of redemption. Of his own free will Christ came to us in a form to which we could relate, with a message that was uncompromised.

Communication: Form and Content

The method used in communicating is extremely important. If the message is to be received as intended, message and

method must agree. The incarnation is highly instructive as a model for that unification.

The incarnation can be seen as the perfect work of art in the sense that there is an indissoluble unity between what Christ had to say and the way he said it. "Form" and "content" supported each other. That is, his life and actions (form) corresponded to what he was and to what he said (content). There was fusion between the two because the content and the form, though separate, were not separated. Incarnationally, they were unified. There was an organic relationship—one falling out of synch with the other would have destroyed or at least distorted the whole. G. William Jones is very persuasive on this matter:

> The question of content, or of what the work communicates to its beholder, is actually inseparable from the consideration of the question of form, or of how the work is constructed. In a truly artistic creation, *what* a work has to communicate and *how* it communicates it are one and the same thing. . . . consider a poorly executed film production in which the producers are concerned only with presenting their message visually and care little about camera placement and movement, lighting, the technical quality of sound recording, and editing. . . . the form of their presentation has not only influenced negatively their intended message, but has actually been part of the content [a negative content] conveyed to the viewer. This perhaps serves to illustrate the mistake of those who endeavor, consciously or not, to separate content from form.[10]

It is quite possible for our method of expressing truth to negate the truth we attempt to communicate. The incarnation teaches us not to divorce what we say from how we say it.

Music is considerably more complicated and involved than visual arts such as film or drama and needs further explanation on this matter of the unity of form and content. Content in music has been variously described on several levels: the musical elements of melody, harmony, texture, rhythm, and so on; the emotional impact of music; the beauty resulting from formal organization; the story suggested by the music (as in program music); the "vision" of the artist; and the intuitive idea (musical or otherwise) of a work. Everything that is communicated to the listener by the musical work can with some validity be called content.

Even in painting, which is not nearly so abstract, a single work may have many levels of content. For example, in a highly abstract painting line, space, and color may be the content. But in another painting who can say that line, space, and color are no longer content merely because the artist has used them to show the pathos inherent in a subject's face? Line, space, and color are still there, and the artist is still concerned with them. They are still content although another level of content has been added. One may see various things in an art work and appreciate it in different ways, depending on what one brings to it in terms of life experience, understanding, talent, and interest. Further, an art work may mean something different to the appreciator than to the artist—a trait of all communication, including verbal communication. Nevertheless, within a given cultural context there will be a general correspondence between maker and knower.

Music, being the most abstract of all the arts, is particularly adept at embracing various meanings simultaneously. Church music entails yet another level of meaning: gospel content. Music cannot physically incarnate the gospel, but it can embody certain traits of the gospel. In doing so church music becomes a musical analogue of gospel content. Church music's form (i.e., its notes, melodies, rhythms, and harmonies, which are the formal rhetoric of music) must faithfully typify the true, the honorable, the just, the pure, the lovely, the gracious, the excellent, and the worthy (Phil 4:8). Then medium and message become incarnate in a beautifully unified musical statement of gospel intent. Music that shows these traits has integrity and adheres to the universal artistic principles of coherence, unity, continuity, dominance, variety, and tendency gratification established by God in creation.

Implicit Communication

Communication is commonly thought of as a process that imposes, more or less strongly, one person's thought upon another—an idea akin to propaganda. Communication thus often becomes imposition, pressing on people what they do not have, as in the Madison Avenue concept of selling. When religion is "sold" it is not uncommon to find great frustration on both sides. The communicator feels thwarted because what is being said may not be "getting across," and the one receiving the communication does not want or understand the message, or else does not like the "package" in which it is wrapped, and so is resentful. The recipient is aware of being exploited and treated as insentient, for exploitation and object manipulation are the essence of communication as propaganda. Obviously enough, propagandizing the gospel perverts it.

On the other hand, the Bible shows incarnational communication to be suggestive, to be implicit. Jesus utilized discovery and dialogue; there were no high-powered selling techniques, sales gimmicks, or slogans. The truth of God does not lend itself to brainwashing or browbeating, and if these are used, the message is inevitably changed. To propagandize a message whose content resists imposition can only result in the distortion of the message. The gospel is not a candidate for the hard sell.

We assume all too readily that music should be patterned after the highly charged verbal barrages to which we are accustomed, but Jesus' usage of such non-explicit techniques as aphorism, parable, parallel, pun, word play, and story suggests that indirect methods of communication are the most appropriate for communicating the church's message. Art and particularly music are therefore especially good means of communicating the gospel, because they work best on the implicit, indirect, and inferential level. A criterion for evaluating music used this way is not the degree to which it pleases (this places too much direct emphasis on the music itself), but the degree to which the musical system is familiar within the general cultural context of its listeners and so can get its message across.

One would be hard-pressed to find an instance when music does not effect some change, however small, in the listener. But in the church we often have the notion that effective communication only happens when music that is pretty, undemanding, popular, and well-liked sweetens the sourness of the text and thus "disarms" the natural resistance of listeners, softening them up for the message. This music is useful to the degree to which it is liked. The greater the liking the better the communication. Musical communication then boils down to serving up what the people like and want to hear, a kind of musical taste treat that turns out to be nothing more than self-indulgence, the pastoral ministry of music acting in the capacity of chef and waiter.

But implicit musical communication is destroyed when the main consideration for choosing music is that it entertain. Music that stirs reflection and invites a free response is much more consonant with Jesus' method of communicating. Church music characterized by decibel overkill, a raucous driving pulse, noisy instrumentation (the trap set!), and hedonistic assimilation should be replaced by a music that exhibits gentleness, contemplation, and thoughtfulness. Incarnational communication is inferential. It calls for the implicit approach. In an age of management and manipulation church musicians could well learn from the methodology of the incarnation.

Summary

The incarnation yields a theological groundwork for the church musician to be humble and ministry pastoral. Furthermore, the incarnation shows that God became relevant in Jesus Christ. Musical relevance is necessary in that the music must be within the general cultural context of the congregation. It is not a matter of likes and dislikes but a matter of familiarity with the general technical musical system of our culture. Music that is completely alien (strange to the point of gibberish) provides no basis for a common understanding and thus denies the incarnation principle. In addition, the incarnation shows that church music's formal value defines its level of gospel content. To witness to the gospel in terms of music is a matter of truth or integrity. Every piece of music in any given church situation communicates a certain degree of affirmation or denial of the gospel. Finally, the incarnation, being an implicit form of communication, gives us necessary insight into the type of communication appropriate for church. We should use a music that is ordinary, not sensational nor laden with overkill.

Our concern should be with music that is appropriate to what it represents, a type of music that invites honest response and active reflection.

As a pastor, the minister of music leads the congregation with love and is concerned with musical standards as they reflect spiritual truth within the context of the assembly. Humility, relevance, form and content, and indirect communication are themes useful and necessary to church music. Each contributes to the larger truth upon which a dynamic music ministry is founded.

5 The Gospel and Contemporary Culture

Before we evaluate some of the more controversial forms of church music today, we should briefly discuss musical witness. As noted in the previous chapter, there needs to be a certain unity or complementarity between music (form) and words (content), between what music says and how it says it. We should not expect the march music of John Philip Sousa to express the sentiment of a tender love poem, nor would the text of "Wouldn't It Be Loverly?," "Houn' Dog," or "Say You'll Be There" be satisfactorily expressed through Gregorian chant. In these cases the music would be so foreign to the idea of the text that gross distortion would result.

The church needs musicians who know what church music should express and who also understand the musical methodology for expressing it. If music is thought of as a kind of lubricant for propaganda purposes, or on the other hand as art isolated and severed from textual meaning and intent, its nature is both misunderstood and underestimated. Good musical witness requires both texts that have something to say, and also music compatible with that message. The words (theology) and music (art) must match.

It is not correct to assume that a particular text can only be expressed by one particular piece of music. Rather, the general category of gospel witness needs musics that are good enough to effectively convey general theological truth. The medium (music) embodies the gospel content indirectly; the text expresses the gospel directly.

Music articulates in a manner similar to words in that every musical medium says something. Marshall McLuhan expressed what musicians have long known—"The medium is the message." The medium (music) is not neutral. It is a dynamic force and deserves careful consideration. As a powerful element in singing, the musical medium either colors and reinforces the words or contradicts them. So compelling is music that it overwhelms the text; so much so that a song does not really belong to the art of poetry or to the art of poetry and music; a song belongs to the art of music. Words are important to church music to give specific thought content to the gospel and must therefore be highly relevant, but the music actually "carries" the song by its ability to represent general gospel content.

The fact that church music defines and articulates general theological meaning makes it mandatory that church musicians understand both the basic complexion of New Testament truth and also how music expresses this truth. All church music, whether congregational songs, choir anthems, solos, or instrumental music, needs to render the underlying thrust or tone of the gospel accurately regardless of the specific and minute details of the text. The characteristics of the gospel must be matched with similar characteristics in the music if the music is to show gospel meaning. In a sense, the music becomes the gospel. It is the gospel in musical attire or musical action.

Gospel Characteristics

Though the attributes of the gospel are many, a few will be discussed in the following paragraphs to ascertain the general feeling or tenor of the gospel. The good news of Jesus Christ is universal in scope but personal in application. Christ died not for the human race collectively but for every human individually. The immeasurable riches of God's grace are sufficient to meet every personal need. In Christ we can fulfill our potential, becoming what no one else has been or will be. Individuals are not reduced to faceless anonymity, nor are they part of a huge, impersonal human collective. Christ knows us by name and gives us the freedom to be idiosyncratic beings. God lives in and through us, yet we are distinct. He does not intend that humans become carbon copies of one another. Each of us is different and is to bring a further and distinct glory to God's capacity for creating uniquely. God's creating is unlike modern mass production techniques. Individual personality remains a very precious part of the creative work of God as shown to us in the gospel of Jesus.

The love of material possessions is a hindrance to the kingdom. The work of the gospel is the antithesis of storing up huge fortunes. For the Christian, possessions are a means for building up the kingdom. Wealth tends to make claims on its possessor. But the believer, in order to do the will of God, must be free and unshackled from any hindrance. The rich young ruler and Ananias and Sapphira are biblical examples of people whose love of money kept them from God's best. The gospel does not tolerate any claim that one of its purposes is the selfish accumulation of earthly things.

The gospel is the key to full creativity, as noted in our discussion of the *imago Dei*. It encourages the full use of the creative gift as human creators fulfill their creative responsibility. In being a Christian, one finds the freedom to be uniquely creative and original. The gospel offers no cosmetic facelift; it runs deep and swift in cleansing and shaping power. It shows the fallacy of superficiality and of being concerned for effect without regard for cause. The gospel of Christ stands for integrity and wholeness. Genuine newness is the result of an inward dynamic at work—a creativity that breaks new ground with imagination and integrity.

The call to sacrifice is part of the gospel. It appears throughout the Bible and culminates in God's ultimate sacrifice of giving his only begotten Son to die a hideous death for our sins. Christ's sacrifice calls us to unwavering devotion to God and sacrifice of self. We cannot escape the fact that our interests must serve exclusively God's call. The Lord calls us to serve, not on the basis of what we might get out of it but on the basis of what we have to give sacrificially.

The gospel costs something in terms of discipleship. Christ's death and resurrection put on those who accept him as Savior a responsibility to give everything we have and everything we are. Such a duty is often difficult, even painful. To be a disciple is to live a life of renunciation, to exist for others, to leave family, lands, possessions, and friends, to make the primary motivation for living doing the will of the Father. There is a cost to such discipleship, and the gospel does not water down the cost, even though there are few, according to the Scripture, who are willing to pay the price. There are no shortcuts, no easy ways, no getting around the fact that discipleship means discipline.

True discipleship, however, brings joy—a deep-seated joy that comes from taking upon oneself the Christ-yoke and by carrying out God's commands as revealed in the gospel. A sense of well-being comes from casting oneself on his love and mercy, from depending on him for life and sustenance, from living in the realm of faith where one's whole being is emotionally and intellectually saturated with the presence of God. This joy is not predicated on earthly circumstances or on human merit, but on what Christ has done. It is therefore changeless and undiminished because Christ is ever the same. The joy of discipleship is a far cry from amusement and entertainment; it is beyond description in its depth, and it colors all that one is and does even in the disappointments and sorrows of temporal life.

The gospel requires the highest standards of living. Before Christ came, murder was prohibited in the Ten Commandments, but Jesus taught that merely hating someone was as bad as the physical act of killing. Further, enemies are to be loved and good bestowed upon persecutors. The Christian has no personal right to avenge wrong. The gospel contains standards of behavior that exceed those of the Old Testament as well as those of civil government. There is no higher or more sweeping code of conduct than that required of the Christian. It must be remembered that God is the source of this standard. His is a heavenly calling, a divine obligation toward which the redeemed are to strive, not in their own strength but in the power of the Spirit.

Integrity is everything to a Christian. Methods and motivations for accomplishing goals are derived from principles found in Scripture. The gospel does not approve of good action apart from right motives. A cup of cold water given because one wishes to be seen by people is contrary to what the Word teaches. Purity of heart and honorable intentions are part of Christian character. Integrity is the scrupulous outward manifestation of the Christian's internal incorruptibility.

The gospel does not teach that life in Christ should be a continual fantasizing for utopia. Such longing, such avoidance of reality, is little more than romantic escape, a type of antinomianism that sees our world as something to be shunned. Jesus' teaching, however, is very much concerned with the here and now. We are not to try and escape the world, but to see it as a gift and a responsibility. To treat life as a burden, so that fleeing reality becomes a prime activity, is to wrap oneself into a shell of romanticism that effectively strips the Christian of the ability to live life fully and well as God intends.

Christ asks the best of each person. "Thou shalt love the Lord thy God with all thy heart, soul, mind, and strength and thy neighbor as thyself" shows nothing slipshod or second-rate about the degree of commitment expected. God demonstrated the level of giving he expects from us by giving his only begotten Son. Jesus was the highest and best gift God could possibly have given. We see this attitude in the exemplary giving of the widow who gave from her poverty everything she had, a gift which in the Lord's eyes was greater than the rich man's because his gift was but a trifle in comparison with his total wealth. The gospel requires nothing less than our all.

Our Lord taught that sensationalism is to be avoided. Praying in the privacy of the prayer chamber is better than praying on the street corner so that people will notice. Whatever is done for the kingdom should not be done for the praise of people. Jesus healed and asked that no one be told about it. The gospel is not something to flaunt but something to work out modestly in living. Christians are to serve quietly, even secretly. The meek way is the gospel way. When good works point to persons, the gospel is violated.

Transience is not a trait of the gospel, for the gospel is changeless. It is given once and for all, and when we take upon ourselves the yoke of Christ, we take it once and for all. It is not a matter of easy come, easy go. To decide for Christ is to accept the fact of a life-long relationship in which the redeemed person is conformed consistently to the image of the Son. The gospel is for the long haul; it is not a modern disposable.

God has made a covenant with humanity that demonstrates his love, mercy, holiness, justice, and power. Humans are total debtors. They bring nothing to the covenant. But in accepting Christ's redemptive work and in becoming new creatures, Christians bring to their regenerated life a responsibility for living out the gospel in all its fullness. Embracing the Christian faith requires doing, and Scripture is a composite body of material that tells each person how to live Christianly. We respond to and show love for God through a thoughtful commitment to the grace of God, costly yet dispensed freely. Dietrich Bonhoeffer has written eloquently about formal Christianity that has no commitment. He says that cheap grace is

> the preaching of forgiveness without requiring repentance, baptism without church discipline, Communion without confession, absolution without personal confession. Cheap grace is grace without discipleship, grace without the cross, grace without Jesus Christ, living and incarnate.[1]

He further compares the costly grace of the gospel to

> the treasure trove hidden in the field; for the sake of it a man will gladly go and sell all that he has. It is the pearl of great price to buy which the merchant will sell all his goods. It is the kingly rule of Christ, for whose sake a man will pluck out the eye which causes him to stumble, it is the call of Jesus Christ at which the disciple leaves his nets and follows him.[2]

The gospel is not to be taken lightly. It is given at great price (the life of Jesus Christ) and received in the same spirit (we give our lives to God). The gospel costs everything. It requires the pathway that people generally try to avoid: the hard way, the disciplined way, the sacrificial way, the lonely way, the way of the suffering servant.

The characteristics enumerated here—drawn in large part from the Sermon on the Mount in Matthew 5–7—indicate a certain basic tenor of the gospel which is of extreme importance, indeed of crucial importance, for the ministry of music.

These traits lead us to the conclusion that one feature of the gospel is an avoidance of popular appeal. Authentic Christianity abhors the enticements of those things that make the gospel over in the image of a fallen world. Easy acceptance and worldly allurement are incompatible with the biblical thrust. The gospel call is one of love *and* one of discipline—a loving discipline that calls us to discipleship and eschews the cushy.

Pop Culture

From time to time I have mentioned our general culture in relation to the church, noting that the church, though part of the totality of culture, transcends culture. This knowledge should inspire the body of Christ to share widely and fully its prophetic word, a word divine in its origin, total in its scope, and ultimate in its finality. Rather than be a passive receiver of culture, or a neutral, nonjudgmental user of culture, it is to mold and "salt" culture, transforming it with precepts, conspicuous and inferred, from the full gospel. A certain discomfort between church and culture should exist. If the church abdicates its cultural duty, its prophetic role is diminished.

We now address these problems between culture and the church. Because some aspects of culture are vividly antireligious, they are easily seen. Consequently believers can strongly oppose them. No Christian needs to be reminded of the church's position on pornography and drug abuse. But the church is too little concerned about other features of culture that appear innocuous but have terribly damaging effects on society and should be subjected to biblical critique: a sweeping relativism that denies the possibility of objective truth; an individualistic selfishness that has become the most elemental substratum of modern existence, affecting literally every discipline, including religion; a hedonistic preoccupation with pleasure, entertainment, and creature comfort; and a commercial approach to life that has influenced notions of making (production) and marketability and transformed entire value systems relating to creativity, quality, desirability, and worth.

Our particular subject of inquiry (pop culture) is just as obscure because of its harmless appearance, its widespread presence, and its general acceptance. Generally its qualities (relativism, selfism, hedonism, and commercialism) are not readily perceived as symptoms of the malaise just briefly described. But taken together, these worldview elements produce an approach to life that is superficial, obsessed with immediate gratification, and oriented around consumer-aligned taste whims. Indeed, it is the main cultural motif of the West and is being exported now to every corner of the globe. To say that pop culture has altered the world's way of life is an understatement. It has revolutionized it.

Pop culture has made substantial inroads into the church, including the pastoral ministry of music. In adopting certain aspects of pop culture that are antithetical to scriptural principles, church musicians have renounced their own prophetic task for the easier one of swimming with the cultural current. The church (and church music is not excluded) must reevaluate its position regarding this perilous stream, and if need be, buck the current, rechannel it, or even dry portions of it up. The church must stop affirming culture passively and uncritically in the name of relevance and accept an active and, when necessary, contravening role that ministers to the whole of life. Hence this twentieth-century cultural development needs further examination. Its characteristics and its influence on the gospel as help or hindrance ought to be assessed.

The phenomenon of pop culture—"kitsch," if you will—has evolved because of centuries (beginning in the Renaissance) of sweeping change in worldview. But the more immediate and obvious progenitor of twentieth-century popular culture is technological innovation—the machine. From steam engine to space rocket, from electricity to electronics, from switch to microprocessor, from animal husbandry to biotechnology, from craft to industry, from hamlet to global village, from music printing to music recording, from music making to music consuming, culture has evolved into the society we know today. Pop culture thrives on a mechanical approach to life. Mass production, mass marketing, and mass media have produced a society in which the overwhelming spirit is one of industrialism and consumption. Individual human autonomy, so highly prized, is largely illusory. Selection, by and large, is limited to a quite narrow range of choices whether in music, politics, TV, religion, etc. Moreover, mechanistic manipulation via information distribution and taste management determine to a large extent the choices made. People are products of their environment. Though they believe they are completely free, in many ways they are as restricted as a computer transistor (on, off) or the piston of a steam locomotive (forward, backward). In large measure, personhood is defined and formed by the engine of technology. Dehumanization, trivialization, and alienation from the past, from tradition, and from the community are common. Men and women become slaves to a lifestyle that is ordered around things. Nothing is exempt. Relationships, work, religion, art, study, and relaxation all gravitate toward a machine orientation that emphasizes speed, quantity, exact timing, technique, and conformity.

Many characteristics of popular culture that stem from technology parallel the methods of industry: standardization, specialization, prefabrication, commercialization, and popularization. We see these traits in the use of averages as prescriptive dogma; in fixations based on unthinking reflexivity; in the continuing trend toward vicarious experience; in the belief that monetary success equals correctness and rightness; and in the assumption that standards based on popular approval have the weight of moral certitude. The fact is that commercialization and a technological way of life, along with the self-centered relativism that denies the possibility of any meaningful concept of truth, have made our society markedly different from any in history.

The arts are not exempt from the influence of popular culture. As a matter of fact, the arts have been in the forefront of the pop revolution. They have promoted pop culture by their own use of and popularization of pop ideals. And as previously intimated, business and industry have found the pop arts lucrative. The music industry customarily denies the charge of market manipulation, but methods of creating demand are fairly well known. First, business knows that the appetites of the public are largely formed by what has been marketed previously. Second, business knows how to create demand for what is about to be marketed. Back in the sixties, H. Radcliff of the Musicians Union maintained that "Any music publisher can tell you six months ahead which tune is going to be popular."[3] While this was a somewhat simplistic generalization, there is overwhelming evidence that the public was manipulated (and continues to be manipulated) far more than it would like to admit. Years later David Willoughby noted that popular music "relies on marketing, advertising, distribution, and sales strategies to manipulate taste and to create and promote hits and star performers. . . . The general public is subject to musical fads, rapidly changing tastes, and manipulation by the media and the music industry."[4]

Commercialization of the arts has lowered artistic standards and encouraged musical tastelessness. People involved in commercial enterprise are indifferent toward the fact that there is a vast difference between true art and the commercialized product. Such a distinction is not particularly relevant in popular culture. The art handicrafter and the mass communicator push the true artist into the background with gimmickry, broad exposure, and business savvy. Popular culture runs on the premise that something is validated through financial gain. After all, one cannot argue with success at the cash register.

Strangely enough, one of the biggest problems in our society is not a dearth of music, but too much. Music of all kinds is used for environmental background. Music then becomes "Muzak."[5] It is not to be listened to with the critical faculties of one's whole person, but simply is to be atmosphere, unobtrusively in the background like pastel colors on a wall. One notices it only when it falls silent. Many Americans rise to mood music, eat to it, drive to it, work to it, telephone to it, entertain to it, shop to it, and go to sleep to it. Background music is simply everywhere. In a scathing attack on this "sewage system of sound," Paul Hindemith shows how damaging it can be to one's listening habits and compares it to brainwashing.[6] It diminishes our musical sensibilities. The environmental use of music dulls and conditions our minds and emotions into a musically unconscious state through the continual barrage of pointless sound.

We not only cease to listen, we cease to hear. We become musically comatose.

> Most of us, surrounded as we are by music almost as inescapably as by air, have successfully pushed it into the background of our consciousness. This is often a matter of simple self-defense. Inferior music beats at our ears in a dreary whine in the home, in stores, and on the streets. Who would wish to listen attentively to this, much less think deeply about it?[7]

This problem has been spawned by technology—specifically, the invention of recording and playback equipment—and by sophisticated merchandising. Business enterprises are formed to make a profit selling musical distribution systems, as well as choosing and programming the musical compositions that are to do "the job." Businesses use mood music because they believe there are beneficial psychological effects on the listener. Companies expect an increase in industrial yield when music is used to alter the work environment. Some churches even go along with pop culture's love affair with background music by installing speakers in every nook and cranny of their building complexes and operating the system almost continually. Even the worship service is not exempt. People who are conditioned to this continual sound become less and less capable of understanding and appreciating art music and develop the psychological problem of being afraid of silence.

The Church and Pop Culture

Popular culture presents the church with many problems. How can the church be in the world yet not be conformed to the world? How can it actively witness to the world but not become identical with it? One answer is by relying heavily on the supernatural in the implementation of its prophetic mission. Aiding in the formation of a healthier culture is very much part of its ministry. But this does not answer the question of what the church's all-inclusive attitude should be toward society. It cannot cut itself off from culture or it will have no ministering place. But it likewise cannot be one with it, for then the church will have nothing prophetic to say. We are to be in the world, but not of the world; the church is caught in the middle. And that seems to be the best answer: to understand the betwixtness and betweenness in a positive way, as a creative counterpoint. There are

> churches which have endeavored to enter into the life of the world and bear witness to the relevance of Christian faith for the totality of human existence without themselves becoming captive to the values and idolatry of the world. Such churches have understood the normative relationship between the church and the world in terms of creative *tension* or polarity.[8]

This tension between the world and the church provides the best climate for fulfilling the Great Commission. Neither an indiscriminate acceptance of culture nor a complete rejection of it is scriptural. Pastorally, the church must not accept cultural forms that are alien to the message it is trying to proclaim. The negative and detrimental facets of pop culture need to be discerned from a biblical perspective. Then appropriate action can be taken based on scriptural principles. True, the church can only witness to culture through cultural forms. That is taken for granted. But it cannot do so uncritically. The distinctives of the gospel must be maintained in the forms used.

Pop Music Characteristics

Pop culture, having had its beginnings in the industrial revolution and its aftermath, has taken a long time to come to its present state, but it has increasingly influenced the development of the arts. It has fostered a whole new genre of music (modern pop) and fostered a whole new way of valuing music (mass appeal). Pop music has in fact become a musical mirror of the heart of our society, the musical embodiment of kitsch. From Tin Pan Alley to gangsta rap, from country to pop rock, from gospel to Contemporary Christian (CCM), popular music is the adopted musical style of Main Street, USA, and beyond, the musical equivalent of the new morality and relativistic thinking, the preeminent musical legacy of the twentieth century.

Of course certain types of "popular" music were in existence long before the advent of the culture of mass appeal.

Indeed, some church musicians are fond of citing Luther's use of *contrafacta* (putting religious words to a preexistent tune, usually secular) as a justification for their use of modern-day pop. But the so called "popular music" of Luther's time and the pop music of our day are two different categories of song; they are as different as night is from day. In the sixteenth century there existed a stylistic unity between the various genres of music that no longer exists: "there was little difference between the features of a melody originally associated with a secular text and one written particularly for a sacred text."[9] "A difference in style between sacred and secular music hardly existed."[10] The popular music of the time had a folk-like character far removed from modern-day pop. Not until the advent of technology did the music that we refer to as pop originate—a twentieth-century expression of a mechanistic worldview.

The word "popular" needs to be defined. Its generic meaning is simply "that which is broadly appreciated." For the sake of clarity, however, I will use the word "popular" as a technical term denoting "made distinctly for widespread acceptance." That is, it refers to what is created to be popular rather than what incidentally has become popular.[11] This usage of the word "popular" refers more to the compositional and aesthetic characteristics of the art form than to the reception of the art form.

The reader needs to be aware that writing about an entire musical genre is necessarily bound to be full of generalizations. Just as every piece written in "classical" style is not of the highest caliber, so every piece of popular music, whether country, rock, or CCM, is not of the same quality. It goes without saying that there are levels of quality within all stylistic categories.

But between major classes of composition, it is erroneous to assume qualitative equality. Some genres are intended to be less artistic and others more so. There is clearly a difference of this kind between twentieth-century popular music and what we might term art music. Pop music's game plan is to be entertaining and fun. It is a light music. While serious music requires careful and principled aesthetic craft, pop music utilizes a more superficial and facile approach. After all, popular music's very success depends upon easy assimilation, ready expendability, commercial banality, and immediate gratification—traits that great music avoids as a condition of its worth.

That having been said, the difficulty of being evaluative and prophetic in relation to this genre should be recognized. Popular music (of all types) is certainly *the* music of our culture. Some of it, such as rock, has become the most popular music not only in the West, but in many eastern and third world countries as well. It is the everyday music of most people, the musical embodiment of the dominant worldview traits of society. Consequently a certain discomfort is bound to result when the validity and suitability of this medium for gospel witness is brought up. But that is the nature of the challenge that faces us. Our fundamental concern here is not the appropriateness of this music for daily consumption (though the reader is encouraged to rethink that question as well) but *the appropriateness of this musical style for use in church.*

So that we might come to grips with this musical form as a setting for religious texts (remember, we seek a unity between the words and the music), we must analyze the characteristics of pop music in more detail. What we wish to discover is how close pop music characteristics are to gospel characteristics. We will then be better able to judge pop music's ability to express the gospel musically. For many people, especially those who have accepted pop as their preferred musical expression, these traits will be obscure, hence generally difficult to identify. Pop tends to limit aesthetic and artistic sensitivity and insightfulness. Nevertheless, the fact that many traits are common to the various styles of pop, and hence highly redundant, gives them visibility.

The most obvious trait of pop music is its prolificacy. Compositions are often approached from a manufacturing standpoint. With limited and short-cut technique they become cookie-cutter copyable. Paul Hindemith, noting pop's proclivity for mass production during the days of Tin Pan Alley, says:

> One shows how denaturized an art can become once it is made a part of an industrial production system totally inhuman and dictatorial. In Hollywood, they keep composers and arrangers in little booths provided

with staff paper and piano, and here on the assembly-line music is produced in which all the normal virtues that are part and parcel of the composer's profession—imagination, enthusiasm, original talent—are just so many factors hindering industrial production.[12]

The commercial assembly line continues to be a normal feature of pop creation. Each part of the work, such as melody, harmony, orchestration, and so on, may be worked on by several people in a group, or farmed out to a "specialist." Arrangers and "arrangements" are common. Rather than carrying through with a complete individual creation, the composer sends it to experts who layer in their area of expertise. These experts perform their work efficiently, albeit one-dimensionally. Holistic integrity and thoroughgoing originality are not particularly mandatory.

Popular music is big business. It is run according to corporate methods and techniques for the sake of huge financial rewards. Full commercialization extends to scientific marketing and popularization procedures for the purpose of influencing taste and creating product demand. The conventions of Tin Pan Alley continue. "Do whatever is necessary to make a sale." Sales are even used as a mark of excellence, recognition of various types being given to the music that sells the best. Pop music gives meaning to the term "commercial banality."

The popular has an incredible drive toward continuous novelty. Durability and depth are not a priority. Wearing out soon, pop must be quickly replaced. In order for it to continue to arrest the attention of the public, pop must endlessly produce new twists, glossed-over clichés, or even outright shock. In its novelty, its shallowness is exposed, for novelty is superficial alteration, a quickly recognizable disguise, change without substance. Novelty is quite often the closest pop as a genre can come to a deep-seated, genuine creativity (that which breaks new ground with imagination and with integrity).

Pop music does not wear well because the actual musical content (melody, harmony, rhythm, form) is fairly standardized. Some authors believe that on the most basic and elemental level there is "nothing inherently different between one 'pop' tune and another."[13] Since pop music's intent is to be purposefully superficial, maximum musical gratification comes immediately. Pop music thus promotes musical immaturity. Our culture, which is concerned with the now and with the self, readily identifies with this pop syndrome because to delay gratification of any kind is anathema. People gravitate toward that which is without cost, without travail, without effort. The demand for things that are immediately gratifying has never been greater. Since it is based on constituent, well worn, tried and true musical conventionalities, some believe pop music's fundamental characteristic is standardization.[14]

Ease of consumption is another aspect of the popular. The art object asks little of the consumer. It is made so that easy assimilation can take place. Thus effort is spared and shortcuts are chosen in order that satisfaction may be achieved directly and conveniently. The presupposition of kitsch is that aesthetic quality be reduced to the level of conventionality. There is little challenge in pop music. If music is to operate on such a popular level, intense music education becomes unnecessary.[15] There is less of musical significance to learn. One can forgo arduous musical discipline because what is made for easy consumption does not require it, either on the part of the composers or on the part of the listeners.

Entertainment is one of the obvious characteristics of pop music. In aiming at pleasure and satisfaction on the immediate level, it dispenses with musical edification. Pop music provides fun and amusement. It need not be concerned with the artistic values characteristic of and necessary to aesthetic beauty. This music's raison d'être is to titillate the emotions, de-emphasizing the intellect. Because it is so pervasive, musical entertainment dominates the musical value system as well as the thought, feelings, and worldview of the consumer. Listeners tend to define reality by the "pleasurable" experiences of pop's hedonism. Modern popular culture "seeks not to encourage reflection, criticism, or discrimination, but to reduce as many serious issues as possible to the level of entertainment."[16] The more society becomes kitsch, the greater the danger of its inability to rise above the lowest common denominator. In many cases, the popular does not merely try for the average, but actively promotes inferiority. The lowest standard becomes the norm. It does this because the path of least resistance requires little of the listener in the way of musical skill or understanding. In requiring little, this music entertains. It encourages musical slothfulness. Stewardship of heart and mind is downgraded. Creativity, integrity, and honesty become but theoretical concepts that encumber amusement. Pop preys upon the Adamic nature. It exploits the human predilection for taking the easy way.

The popular is success-oriented. Success is measured in terms of numerical statistics (which ultimately translate into dollars). Without success the popular has no support and dies a quick death. Thus a basic aim of the popular must be to do only what will appeal—generally what is musically safe for the greatest number of people. The overriding concern is profit, and when that begins to decline, the musical piece withers and dies. It stands not on its own artistic merits but on its ability to sell. There is nothing as stone cold as yesterday's pop hit if it is not producing revenue.

There are elements of romanticism in the popular. Pop music tends to retard emotional maturity and invite unrealized idealization. The characteristics of romanticism in literature, delineated by C. S. Lewis, are themes similarly found in the popular arts: the dangerous or adventurous; the marvelous, the larger-than-life; the abnormal; the selfish and the subjective; the rebellious in respect to civilization or convention; sensitivity to natural objects; intense longing, prized for itself, for that which is unattainable; and mystery in the thing longed for.[17] In music, the pop field is more concerned with fantasy than with reality. Further, vulgarity, violence, and immorality in pop songs have increased dramatically in recent years. Some rock texts, for example, are so abhorrent that even the most liberal newspapers and magazines will not print them. Yet thousands and thousands of people, including children and teenagers, regularly ingest such pop art every day as a matter of course.

The popular creates an environment unfavorable to quality. Great artists refuse to acquiesce to the popularisms and clichés of their day because artistic integrity is incompatible with popularistic appeal. The true artist's purpose is not to find a comfortable berth in the world or to achieve popular recognition, but to get his creative work done.[18] Mediocrity, however, is acceptable to the popular. The commercial music industry must offend as few people as possible in each market segment. This results in a middle-of-the-road approach to art in which the highest artistic value is sacrificed to run-of-the-mill convention. When one creates something to be popular, uniqueness and aesthetic excellence are depreciated. The thing that flourishes in pandering to the marketplace is mediocrity.

The popular capitalizes on sensationalism. Outlandish clothing, obnoxious grooming, psychedelic light displays, electronic modification and augmentation, decibel overkill, and stage gimmicks are often an integral part of musical presentation. The popular is not only vulgar, but it encourages fantasies of grandeur, appeals to the sensuous; it exaggerates and uses extravagance and infantilism. Hyped-up performance is much more important than the inherent quality of the art form. In pop music, slicked-up arrangements are standard fare.

The popular is the epitome of transience. Pop music cannot be anything else, for to be popular is to affirm expendability. The Top 40 hits change regularly, wearing thin very quickly. Having little depth, the popular must depend on its disposability to continue the genre. Though older pop pieces are occasionally brought back, their return is generally motivated by nostalgia for some bygone era.

Many of these popular music qualities stem from the drive to make this art form primarily a means of monetary gain, which is to say that its overall quality is to be found in the area of commercialization. In very direct language, Arthur Korb states that popular music is "written and published primarily to make money."[19] A pop composer treats his music not as an art but as a commodity:

> A [popular] song writer must learn to become a businessman—a clever businessman who will handle himself successfully and make the cash registers keep on ringing up the sales. Your songs are a commodity that you will be placing on the selling market.[20]

> The phrase, "general and immediate appeal to the widest audience" is in fact not only a description of the pop song; it is also a definition of

the word *commercial,* and it's a phrase you better get your teeth into right now. Publisher experience over the years shows that the pop type of tune has the widest appeal, as proved by hard cash over the counter. All pop tunes are therefore commercial. They are the most saleable in the market, the most "popular" (which gives you the origin of the word *pop*).[21]

Monetary reward is the driving force behind the creation of pop music. Artistic integrity gives way to commercial success. To write pop music successfully, composers must strive to write music that pleases the widest audience. Artists are no longer able to freely create, for every creative impulse must be checked by, "What will they think?," "Will they like it?," and "Will it sell?" Writing by convention is much easier than starting from scratch on each new composition. Many popular song writers (sometimes those with the most number of "successes") are technically unable to read music, let alone write it. They fall into the pattern popularized by some pop composers of the 1890s who "composed" by stock melodic, harmonic, and rhythmic formulation. A knowledge of music theory was unessential for mass producing what the public was eager to buy and then inevitably to discard.

> The very climate of the pop music business discourages the nurturing of skill and inspiration. There is a built-in expendability both of materials and artist—neither is expected to last the pace for long.[22]

But the sacrifice of artistic integrity to create pop music is too high a price for an artist to pay. It is tantamount to selling one's artistic soul. The loss of creative incorruptibility brings artistic death.

It is important to mention that simplicity is not necessarily a characteristic of the popular. In our complex technological society, that which is simple is often automatically placed in a "light" or "popular" category. It is true that much pop music is simplistic (and much of it sounds complex due to such devices as the drum machine, amplifier, synthesizer, and other electronic gadgets). However, great music can also be simple. Complex and simple are not analogous to artistic and popular or to good and bad.

Like "popular," the word "contemporary" is often used to describe modern-day religious pop. This is a misnomer, however. "Contemporary" is best used as a technical term describing any musical form whose compositional elements (harmony, rhythm, melody, counterpoint) are characteristic of twentieth-century theoretical practice. It is confusing to consider both Daniel Pinkham and Bill Gaither, for example, as composers of "contemporary" music. True, both are twentieth-century writers, but their individual classifications of compositional technique are quite different—the former is based in the twentieth century (hence contemporary) and the latter, like most composers of religious pop, is based in the functional harmony of the nineteenth century, with some modifications of course. It is likewise confusing to consider "Contemporary Christian Music" a contemporary music in the theoretical sense. Though it is currently being written (and like Gaither, contemporary in that way), the musical essence of most CCM is not based (as the CCM label infers) on twentieth-century theoretical practice and style. It would be more accurate to call this music Religious Commercial Pop or RCP.

Much more could be said about the whole popularistic, mechanistic, technological business syndrome, but for our purposes enough has been mentioned to get at the question of the validity of pop for use in a pastoral ministry of music. We have noted that pop music is concerned with quantity, monetary profit, novelty, immediate gratification, ease of consumption, entertainment, the lowest common denominator, success, romanticism, mediocrity, sensationalism, and transience. Its basic impetus and overall quality is to be found in the drive for making money through musical amusement and musical entertainment. It is a commercial music. One can see in these characteristics a definitive relationship to the characteristics of popular culture. Clearly, pop music is the musical articulation of pop society.

On the other hand, the gospel is concerned with individuality, nonmaterialism, creativity, sacrifice, discipleship, joy, high standards, principles, reality, encouragement of the best, meekness, and permanence. Its overall thrust is a free salvation that opens to everyone a joyous life of loving selflessness and discipline in which the redeemed cheerfully do the will of the Father. The gospel was not made for popular approval or widespread acceptance, for "narrow is the way and few there be who find it."

If these two sets of characteristics were placed side by side they would look like this:

Gospel Characteristics	Pop Music Characteristics
Individual uniqueness	Quantity and standardization
Nonmaterialism	Monetary profit
Creativity	Novelty
Sacrifice	Immediate gratification
Discipleship	Ease of consumption
Joy	Entertainment
High standards	Least common denominator
Principles	Success
Reality	Romanticism
Encouragement of the best	Mediocrity
Meekness	Sensationalism
Permanence	Transience

It is readily apparent from the above list that the gospel characteristics are at odds with those of pop music. Consequently we are driven to the conclusion that if music is to be analogically related to the gospel and to religious song texts, it should not be of the pop variety. Pop and gospel do not mix well. Popular music minimizes musical goodness to achieve popularity and widespread acceptance. The gospel affirms gospel goodness at the expense of popularity and widespread acceptance. To try to force a gospel text into a pop music mold is to force it into something that it is ill-suited to occupy. It seems reasonable to conclude that to use pop music as a medium for the gospel message is erroneous. It is erroneous because the music has adopted characteristics that are contrary to what the words mean. The pop music medium dilutes the message.

The Church and Pop Music

The pop music syndrome has been part of the church music field for over a century. Beginning with the stock formula gospel song, pop style has gradually become the most important single artistic influence on church music. Now at the beginning of the twenty-first century the vast majority of music in evangelical churches and much music in other churches has been patterned after the music of the pop world. Of course, if the whole point of the church and the gospel were popularity, then there would be no other way to go musically. However, this is not the mission of the church.

Church pop is music that has exactly the same musical qualities as "secular" pop. There is a general aura of superficiality in which rhythmic, harmonic, and melodic elements are blended into the kind of musical banality. Quite often such music enters the church long after its introduction into the general music scene, for in the church's lack of genuine creativity it has not even the acumen to copy the world until the new pop becomes "old hat." Such was the case with rock music, for example. For a time it was considered off-limits, even sinful.[23] Converted rock musicians often went around preaching against it. Yet they hurt their own cause by eschewing all aspects of rock (texts, graphics, lifestyles) except the actual music itself! Their lack of musical and theological understanding aided in the eventual acceptance of rock by most churches. Rock became but one of the many popular stylistic bases that churches could choose. And usually the church's rock tended to be derived, quite behind the latest innovations and fads of secular rock. Frankly, it would have been better to leave rock where it was to be what it was.

Pop music (music created to be popular, thus affecting its musical characteristics) is so widespread that many musicians and churches use nothing else. There are children growing up in church who will never know the Christian faith in music as anything but crowd-pleasing musical privation. The convoluted irony of this is that they do not realize it because they have never heard anything else, while many creators of such musical inferiority are well aware of what great church music is. One of the composers of the now-forgotten "folk" musicals, in remarks before a denominational church music conference, noted that

> What we are doing is not necessarily great music. It is music that does work. And it is music that does seem to bring about results. But we . . .

realize that there is great, great music which you should be performing with your young people.[24]

The great tragedy is that though composers of church pop often realize the worth of great music, their pragmatic rationale for composing pop ("doing what works") becomes the local music director's rationale for performing it. This rationale then propagates itself cyclically, with the result that pop exterminates better musical expression. The token performance of an *a cappella* motet or a Bach chorale is not the answer. In such circumstances music of quality is looked upon as medicine taken to appease the musical "highbrows" in the congregation. Great music does not become a normal mode of musical expression. The way of least resistance is to omit anything of musical significance, shortchanging the entire assembly, from children to adults.

The local music director and individual congregation do not carry the full responsibility for such a deplorable situation, though certainly they share part of the blame. Powerful business influences at work within our society (a society already enamored of popular culture) create such irresistible market forces that the Christian church is swept off its feet. The music merchandised is readily apprehensible, light, attractively packaged, and entertaining. Pop musicians jet around the country singing and playing religious concerts complete with advance team, local organization, recordings, and autographed pictures. They mount publicity campaigns and media blitzes to rival that of many political candidates. Press releases, conferences, and interviews give the performer wide exposure and stardust class. Sound tracks, recordings of the most recent worship and praise music as practiced by well-known groups, vocal arrangements, and publisher-sponsored reading sessions with powerful selling techniques increase this music's influence on the entire church. Little by little the church comes to consider such a situation normal. Could popular acclaim be wrong? "One can hardly argue with success," we are told. The accolades and adulation of the crowd, the respect of the public, the gratitude of the clergy, the crowded schedules, the growing importance of the booking agent, all serve to validate pop stars and pop music. Is it any wonder the church wilts under such prestigious influence?

Unfortunately this scenario is played out variously on both larger and smaller scales. The "give them what they want" of pop music finds its way into every musical endeavor. Religious publishing firms, often castigated for being mainly interested in profits, obviously do not bear total culpability for church music's dependence on pop, but they should take seriously some small obligation to help the church in a more responsible way. If they only supply what sells best without attempting to publish better music for a more mature ministry of music (even if it is not on the best-seller list), then the accusation is justified. An inbred loop of supply-creates-demand sets in, and mature musical ministry is inhibited.

CCM singers might also see their work more honestly as entertainment. People who glamorize and idolize these pop entertainers and their music should understand that pop is basically an entertainment music and then attempt to open minds and hearts to other possibilities for music in the church. The difficulty is that popular music expressions tend to create an addiction to entertainment music. It is unlikely that alternatives which require discipline and delayed gratification of listeners would be truly and completely satisfying to them, especially at first. Once pop is in the driver's seat, it is difficult to replace it.

Hence directors of music need to apply all their skill and do everything they can to help congregations become less dependent on this music. By carefully programming music of greater spiritual and aesthetic depth, and gradually removing shallower music, they can make a beginning. While popular "ratings" of directors who implement such a plan may very well go down, it is nevertheless incumbent upon them to try to bring a more mature level of musical and gospel appropriateness to church music. If there is anything at all to this matter of music as ministry, the prophetic thrust of Scripture concerning Christ and culture must not be squelched. Because they deal in musical symbols more than verbal ones, directors must come to grips with musical language first and foremost, since that is music's specific and special way of being the truth, of witnessing to the gospel of Christ.

Truth and Methods

What about the thousands of blessings, conversions, and deeper commitments effected by the world of pop? After all, if it works does not that prove its validity? Surely the church needs every advantage it can get. It is often argued that because people can make nothing qualitatively worthy of God anyway, they need not worry about quality at all. Why struggle and strain against the stylistic and qualitative conventions of pop? Since we cannot do anything intrinsically worthy of God, since pop is a favorite, albeit trivial, music, and since it works, why should we question its use?

These questions are among the first to be heard whenever there is a difference of opinion on the use of pop music in church. In our pragmatic, success-oriented society, the preponderant hypothesis is that whatever brings people to faith, or disposes people positively toward God is not only all right but should be actively promoted. However, if results were always driven by pragmatism, all culture, including religion, would depend more on human nature and our fallen state than upon biblical principles, which often cut across the grain of mortal ways of doing things. Yet pragmatism is rampant.

Good results can be attained with incorrect methods. For example, Moses was instructed by God to speak to the rock for water to quench the thirst of the children of Israel; instead he disobeyed and smote the rock with his rod. Water still came—he got the desired result. An extreme example is Judas, who carried out a most despicable act of betrayal leading to the crucifixion of our Lord, which made salvation possible. Nevertheless both were held responsible by God for their acts—even though their actions were used to bring about God's plan.

God is sovereign. He can use anything to bring glory to his name and to accomplish his will: the disobedience of Moses, the infidelity of Judas. He can use whatever pittance we give him. But this does not excuse us from right conduct. St. Paul did not encourage the Roman Christians to continue in sin that grace might abound that much more. "God forbid," he said. People are still responsible for their actions and will have to answer for them, good results or not! Because of his disobedience, Moses was prohibited from entering the promised land. Judas went out and hanged himself. The fact that God's sovereignty is not dependent on right human action is no reason to think that God is uninterested in methodology. He is simply not bound by it. If he were, he would not be God. Therefore, the fact that something "works" is more a statement about God's sovereignty and his use of what we in our human poverty provide him than a validation of the particular method or practice in question.

Church music methodology should be based on scriptural principles. Right methods are absolutely vital. They validate our witness. The Bible itself, a book of God's self-disclosure in history, was given to teach us how to live. We are to carry through its principles in all of life—even in our music. The music of ministry must have the qualities of that which it hopes to impart. Musical communication that is musically honest and good has much more in common with the gospel than music that is musically hackneyed and cheesy. Hucksterism and musical enticement are not justifiable. Obedience to godly precepts results in the use of a well-constructed and fully creative music. The gospel principles enumerated earlier should not be musically conformed to this world, but should be transformed into the musical essence of those gospel principles. Methods are in human hands—results are in God's.

Church musicians are going to have to answer for their methods even as Moses did. The gospel does not support unbridled pragmatism. Though pop works well as entertainment, its technical characteristics limit its use as church music. Musicians need to be especially discriminating in their choices. Our culture desperately needs an alternative to the selfistic incurvature of immediate gratification.

Folk Music and Jazz

There are two other types of musical expression that should be briefly examined, for they often come up in the same context as pop music—folk music and jazz. Folk music has always been a distinct part of human culture. It has influenced art music of all ages, sometimes as a moderating influence, sometimes as raw material for musical composition, sometimes as the genesis for theoretical experimentation.

Folk music must be sharply distinguished from popular music of the type under consideration in two important respects. First, folk music arises primarily from within a particular culture, often without known composers. It may have a variety of purposes, but it is predominantly a utilitarian music; it is part of the tapestry of daily life. It is not music to eat by or to listen to in a concert hall. It is music to participate in. Thus arises a body of music that has wide acceptance, grows and changes slowly, and shows the primal thought of its culture about such things as birth, death, love, work and play, success and failure, hope and despair.

The second distinguishing mark between folk music and pop music is the absence of commercialism in the former. Folk music has no "professional composers" and is not a music for the purpose of making a profit. It is not a commodity. Therefore, its popularity does not rest on its being made in a certain way so that it will be popular. There is no thought of "doing things" to the art form for predetermined ends. Folk music is popular in the sense that it is of the people and not foisted on the people. It is part of the evolutionary process of culture. The integrity of the music lies in its faithful mirroring of common musical usages.

Folk tunes have often been used as raw material for more popular musical expressions. Roy Harris noted:

> When Broadway seemed to be running out of material, some of the smart songwriters decided to make a raid on the virgin soil of American primitive folk song. Today the air waves are flooded with commercial versions of old folk tunes set to June-moon-swoon rhymes, sung by confection-mike voices accompanied by slick bands.[25]

Such procedures as significantly changing the rhythm to make a tune a bit more "catchy," changing or adding harmony, or rewriting the tune are often used. By the time some folk songs have been thoroughly rehashed, the face-lifting is so complete that the original freshness, spontaneity, and down-to-earth quality have been completely incinerated.

It is tempting for people to "sophisticate" this music, to "make it better." Folk music has been subjected to all types of manipulation. Such well-meaning attempts often end up vulgarizing a perfectly valid medium. Routley shows that Geoffrey Beaumont's "Folk Mass," the granddaddy of religious "commercial folk," is not folk music at all except for a few passages.[26] Such forms as "folk-musicals," "folk-rock," and "gospel-folk" were slicked up renditions of the folk style. Such adaptations and others like them show themselves to be much more commercial and pop than "folk." Occasionally, the term "folk" was adapted solely for the purpose of sales appeal. Such pieces had very few of the musical characteristics of folk but abounded in pop manifestations.

Folk songs are usually strophic, sometimes modal, often rhythmically free, and predominantly monophonic. They have been influential in the development of western music from its inception, even bearing upon the evolution of chant.[27] Their greatness is in their utter simplicity. Artlessness is their strength. Folk music is never pretentious, sensational, or maudlin; it is earthy and wholesome.

Folk music seems to be an ideal form of religious music. It shows unique traits of creativity that are fresh and vital. The music, being music of integrity, is able to carry the Christian message well. Its simplicity and directness add to its usefulness. In a sense, the gospel is utterly simple so that a child can receive it, and folk music emphasizes this aspect of the gospel better than any other music. It also musically portrays the wide invitation for all to come to Christ, for folk music, because it is a music of all people, does not have any hint of being highbrow or lowbrow; it is appreciated by the educated music lover as well as by the uneducated. Many recent hymnals have included an increase in the number of folk tunes from around the world. Folk music's usefulness continues.

Another musical genre that often comes up in the context of popular music is jazz. André Hodeir, in chronicling its history, says that jazz has gone through an artistic evolution.[28] New forms, building on old forms, were continuously improved, so that creative jazz, which began as musically uninteresting material, gradually became music of artistic merit and genius. Leonard Bernstein wrote:

> The jazz player has become a highly serious person. He may even be an intellectual. . . . He may have studied music at a conservatory or a university. This was unthinkable in the old days. Our new jazzman plays more quietly, with greater concentration on musical values, on tone quality, technique. He knows Bartok and Stravinsky, and his music shows it.[29]

Jazz is an indigenous American genre and must be considered to have achieved the state of a serious art form. Indeed the harmonic and contrapuntal foundations of "creative" jazz are extremely intricate and the performance requirements so high that only the technically competent are able to play this type of music well. Jazz, therefore, is musically definable and has become a great musical expression in its own right.

Jazz, like folk music, must be distinguished from our definition of pop music. As modern jazz developed into serious musical expression, it found difficulty in achieving

> popularity without forsaking the achievements of modern jazz. Since the end of the war only a very few jazz musicians—and not always the best—have managed to find favor with the general public who, in any case, prefers the howling idols of rock 'n' roll.[30]

Jazz has achieved the status of art music at the expense of popularity. To try for mass appeal, contemporary jazz would have to sacrifice the values and principles that have made it great. We must conclude that popular music and jazz are far from being the same thing, for jazz is much richer than pop, both aesthetically and emotionally.

Like all music, jazz is uneven in quality. Some of it is very bad, showing pop traits. But it is a relatively young expression, and as it develops along the lines of integrity, more and more of it will be adaptable to situations calling for greatness. Having musical worth, good jazz is compatible with the gospel because it is good art.

> In their encounter with jazz, Christians may embrace it as part of their culture, part of the goodness of God's created world. But unlike pop music, it is not merely a commodity designed for consumption; its purpose goes deeper than escape or entertainment.[31]

Nevertheless its use in church music remains problematic. For many people, the word "jazz" conjures up a picture of smoke-filled dance floors, dimly lit bars, and scantily dressed waitresses. For a congregation that makes such negative connections, jazz obviously cannot be the powerful expression of gospel witness that it might be. Then too, jazz is a specialized music. Being improvisationally based, it is not practical for use with a congregation. While some choral pieces and instrumental arrangements are available, most of them tend toward a certain entertainment-like superficiality. But jazz renditions that are truly creative, not based on convention or cliché (compositionally or instrumentally), can be spiritually edifying if performed well.

Summary and an Urgent Theological Resolve

The period in which we live has been characterized as post-modern, post-Christian, post-moral, and so on. But these designations do not describe what culture has become, just what it has moved beyond. The contention of this chapter is that when all the "posts" are added together, when the move toward relativism and extreme pluralism, selfism, hedonism, and materialism is analyzed, when what is valued most highly is noted, the adjective "popular" or "pop" describes contemporary culture to a tee.

The spirit of pop is to be found in the syndrome of trivialization, simplism, reduction to an average, reduction to a formula, mass production, commercialization, and broad dissemination. Industry and machines are important in popular culture. Technology has come to play an increasingly large role in the musical world, not only in the mechanical dissemination of music, by means of compact disks, tapes, listening systems, MTV, radio, and the ever-present Walkman and boombox, but also in the mechanical manipulation of music in the recording studio. Note popular culture's influence on pop music as it combines musical superficiality, production-line method, and commercialization. Society, including the church, has become comfortable with music that is below par, acceptance often taking place unconsciously. For example, a century ago many branches of the evangelical church embraced the pop-style gospel song. Thousands of these religious songs were mass produced, published, and marketed so that entire generations were brought up solely on the tunes of "In the Garden," "The Old Rugged Cross," "At the Threshold,"[32] and "Shall We Gather at the River?" What they were brought up with became the standard to be perpetuated. Only during the late 1950s and the 1960s, and only after much travail, did many evangelical churches reluctantly admit new musical expressions. Even then it was the newer pop styles that made most of the inroads. Today pop stylistic elements, performance practices, and educational methods—and pop's characteristic elevation of technology over art—continue to gain ground at an increasing rate.

Those in the pastoral ministry of music must make a conscious effort to affirm worthier and truer musical expressions and to return pop to its rightful place within our culture. Music, like the gospel, can never come cheap or easy, either in its creation or in its appreciation. Pop traits and gospel traits are antithetical. Church music must affirm creativity and discourage commercial banality as it impacts culture. Let the church scatter the salt of the gospel with artistic wholeness and integrity, something pop is inherently unable to do well. The message is *in* the medium.

6 *Faith*

The theme of faith is familiar to all churchgoers. Every believer has at some time been exhorted to "have faith," to "move mountains." Our treatment of the term will be broader than this. Here, the word "faith" will be used in two interdependent ways: (1) as a general mode of Christian being, and (2) as a specific type of action. The first, faith as a general mode of being, refers to the Christian faith, the life of faith, the life in faith, living the Christian life. The second, faith action, involves stepping into the unknown, walking blindly in the absolute certainty of one's trust in God.

The Wholeness of the Christian Life

The life of faith (i.e., the first of the two meanings of faith just delineated) is a fundamental attitude or outlook on life in which a Christian's worldview has been centered on the Creator. The resulting worldview is holistic. The world is neither something to be cursed nor something to be resigned to. The regenerate should see all of life as a gift to be developed for glorifying the Creator. The Christian faith puts together the fragmented pieces of life as the believer comes to know purpose and meaning. With a perspective derived from Christ, all of life manifests the eternal and corroborates the central thesis that God is the Creator who loves us, has redeemed us, has promised us healing, and has given the world to us as a gift and a responsibility.

The Christian's life, then, is a wholly integrated existence. There must be no barriers, no imbalances, no compartments.

All of life is lived in Christ and everything the Christian does is centered on this perspective. As Herbert W. Farmer has said, the Christian life is "the massive unity."[1]

Two problems in church music illustrate the widespread assault on the wholeness of the Christian life. The first problem is the sacred-secular bifurcation. The second problem is the imbalance of emotion and reason in music and in religion.

First, the unity of life lived in faith may be fragmented by a sacred-secular dichotomy in which some parts of existence are believed to be under the domain of the sacred while others are believed to be the province of the secular. These boundaries are artificial. For the Christian, nothing falls outside the unity of the life in faith. If anything touches life, it is part of one's faith life. All that the redeemed are and all that they do is under the authority of the sacred because Jesus Christ is the source and center of all Christian living.

Historically the church has been concerned with sacred-secular issues regarding its music. The early church fathers attempted to be very clear in their pronouncements on such matters. Their aim was to keep the church's music from pagan and undue secular influence. But through the centuries the church, often misunderstanding the nature of artistic development, frequently prohibited worthy musical creativity by relying on legalistic regulations to screen its music. The result has been to retard consistent musical progress in the church. Many fine musical developments outside the mainstream of church life were assimilated only with great reluctance (howbeit steadily and systematically) at the insistence of composers. Today any such determination to keep "secular" music out has largely evaporated—and rightly so, philosophically and theologically speaking. What confronts the church at present is the recurring question of style and quality. It must be added, however, that in some quarters even the question of style is a dead issue, all musical styles (yes, all) being considered legitimate for use in music ministry!

Actually, one is at a loss to explain what it is that is supposed to make music in and of itself sacred or secular. The usual explanations, such as words, style, compositional devices, sincerity, artistic value (or lack of it), and religious orientation of the composer, are all ultimately unsatisfactory. Paul Henry Lang has shown that it is impossible to establish a set of rules for making music "sacred" and therefore suggests that the term be avoided.[2] After all, the stuff of music (time and tone) is not religious or profane but amoral. If the raw material of music cannot be considered sacred or secular then the finished product in and of itself is "neither sacred or secular; it is only interesting or dull, polyphonic or monophonic, accompanied or *a cappella,* and so on."[3] However an important caution is in order. The fact that music is intrinsically neither sacred nor secular does not mean all music is suitable for church. Far from it. Some music is inherently unsuitable, not because it is secular but because of other considerations: its worldview, its quality, its general style or aura, or its appropriateness in a given situation.

"Sacred" and "secular" are not qualities of things; they are qualities of relationships. For example, one cannot paint a Christian landscape, but one can view it in a Christian way. Thus the terms "sacred" and "secular" are better used in conjunction with a mode of existence—namely one's basic orientation as either sacred or secular, holy or profane. For the Christian, life in its entirety is sacred. There are no compartments; work, recreation, relationships, art, and music are seen through life in Christ.

This is not to suggest that church music standards should be abolished and all music judged equally fit for church music ministry—far from it! But a recognition that sacred-secular classifications are not qualities of things (compositions) opens up for many congregations new possibilities, such as the great masterworks of musical art. It also gives a unification and a Christian purpose to all of one's music making. Musical choice will not be made on the basis of sacred-secular categories but on music's ability to stand the scrutiny of musical-theological judgments. What is worthy will be retained and what is unworthy will be discarded. The result will be a comprehensive music-life unity in which the life in faith from beginning to end, from top to bottom, in and out, through and through, will be seen as wholly consecrated—in a word, "sacred."

With respect to the second problem, the imbalance of emotion and reason, it must be said that humans consist of mind and emotion in an inseparable unity. Dividing people into isolated segments as we are so prone to do gives a distorted picture of the wholeness that is a God-given characteristic. Humans know and feel; they feel and know. Mind acts upon emotion, and emotion upon mind. Each contributes equally to the making of the complete person. Without this balance, gross distortion results. Emotion and mind together constitute the necessary balance.

The redemptive purposes of God include the whole of a person's being, for the gospel creatively opens the channels of both the intellect and the emotions. The gospel affects everything that makes up an individual. The Christian who is living the life of faith knows the gospel to be "good news for the *whole* man, not just for some department of his being or activity."[4] Christ touches the furthest reaches of existence.

The arts, too, address the whole person, requiring the integrated use of mind and emotion. They demand all of the human personality, both in making and in appreciating, for as many philosophers and aestheticians have noted, art speaks to mind and emotion simultaneously. Music in particular is a complex activity related to a vast number of phenomena. Even music's two fundamental schools of aesthetic thought—the autonomous, with its emphasis on reason (music has no meaning beyond its own intrinsic worth), and the heteronomous, with its emphasis on emotion (the meaning of music is extramusical)—cannot stand alone. Each gets at only one side of the truth; they are correctives to each other. Charles Hoffer notes that "it is nearly impossible for anyone to separate intellect and emotion when listening to music" and that "composers don't write one piece to be heard intellectually and another emotionally."[5] Music is a unity and there can be no dividing it up:

> Music is not merely a succession of pleasing sound-patterns formed of sensuous tone but is essentially an utterance of the whole man. Its message is not primarily addressed either to the intellect or to the emotions, but to the complete personality of the listener; and the

message, to be valid, must spring from the complete personalities of both composer and performer.[6]

To see how music can strengthen and express the holistic life of faith, we must further investigate the role of intellect and emotion in both religion and music.

There is an intellectual side to religion, though often it is mistrusted and thought of either as incidental or as a necessary affliction. Particularly in evangelical Christianity, where emotion is considered primary, are there covert and sometimes overt attempts to discredit mind. In recent years liberal theology has also promoted a more visceral, experiential approach to religion. However, an encounter with God is always accompanied by intellectual activity. People must involve mind in order to believe; without it they cannot come to God, or think of him, or understand the Word. If intellectual activity is omitted, or even slighted, a distorted picture of God's revelation results. To repudiate mind and concentrate on emotion is to sentence the believer to an existence based on unpredictable feelings. Christians living the life of faith as it was intended cannot live this way.

Music, like religion, is very much an intellectual affair, but this view has many critics as well, particularly among those who see music as primarily emotive. The nineteenth-century musical commentator and aesthetician Eduard Hanslick nobly battled the view—preponderant in that day—that music's whole purpose is to create pleasurable emotions in the listener. In our own century, Igor Stravinsky emphasized the intellectual side of music. He believed that music had too long been subjected to extramusical associations. For him, music was primarily an activity of the mind, and its purpose was to be itself. He says:

> I consider that music is, by its very nature, powerless to *express* anything at all, whether a feeling, an attitude of mind, a psychological mood, a phenomenon of nature, etc. . . . If, as is nearly always the case, music appears to express something, this is only an illusion, and not a reality.[7]

Paul Hindemith and Aaron Copland also emphasize music's intellectuality, though neither would discount its power to be emotionally expressive. Hindemith held that listening on the intellectual plane was a matter of mentally reconstructing the inner workings of musical components and that such an ability was necessary for full artistic appreciation of music. Copland thought that listening on the musical (intellectual) level was important enough to write a book about it, *What to Listen for in Music.* His book explains the constituent parts of music in a way that even the nonmusician can understand clearly and logically.

> To listen intently, to listen consciously, to listen with one's whole intelligence is the least we can do in the furtherance of an art that is one of the glories of mankind.[8]

One must listen with the mind in order to really hear, in order to perceive the "contours and inner lines, the lights and the shades, the rhythms and colors, and the constructional components."[9] The ear of reason is the basis of rational understanding.

Without question, then, it seems that both creating music and appreciating music are intellectual activities. How much one emphasizes the intellectual aspects depends upon individual knowledge. For example, musicians and aestheticians, who are aware of formal beauty as a result of careful thought, are apt to accentuate listening as a mental activity. Yet no musical composing, performing, or creative listening of any depth will take place without substantial use of the intellect. The composer-creator mind must be met by a listener-creator mind. Music, like faith, demands the use of reason.

Evangelical Christianity has accepted emotion much more readily than intellect. "Giving one's heart to Christ" is a common theme. The well-known bias for feeling is seen historically in the emphasis placed on emotion in the camp meeting, tent revival, and sawdust trail, as well as in the modern phenomena of Pentecostal and charismatic worship.

God made us passionate creatures. The redemptive gift is applicable to every part of being, including emotions. Worship can be fervent, even impassioned, because we have the capacity to love and feel deeply. Christians have experienced God's warmth, understanding, and divine love in the giving of Jesus

Christ to be the propitiation for sin, in the record of Christ's dealings with God's people, and in the personal relationship believers have with the Son.

> In short, the divine as revealed in the Word can be an object of worship precisely because it can be the object of human emotion. And man can be an object of God's grace because he is an object of divine emotion.[10]

The Bible emphasizes this warm, personal relationship between God and individual by using anthropomorphic and anthropopathic words. But as we have previously intimated, the ultimate example of the intensity of God's love for his human creation is the incarnation. God loves passionately. His love should be received and reciprocated in kind.

According to the biblical record, the emotions are important, particularly in relation to the human heart as the seat of affective life, and are seen as needing redemption by virtue of being part of human nature. The emotions form a significant avenue of expression of praise and worship to the Creator. Religion cannot neglect human emotion. God is a feeling God—through Christ he seeks impassioned followers.

"To believe" often implies dry intellectual assent to religious propositions. But once belief becomes emotional, clothed in warmth and passion, it becomes living faith. The life lived fully in faith is aware of the need to give the heart its rightful place as that which energizes the intellect. Emotion is not to be shunned. It is the fire of the faith life.

The biased notion that music only expresses emotion is so widespread that many musicians are tempted to concur. And in fact, though music has other aspects as well, psychological tests have proved without question that it does influence the affective state of the listener.

What one brings to the musical encounter by way of taste, background, age, interest, musical experience, and association, will in large measure determine the emotional quality of the listener's response. To the degree that these items are similar, responses between persons tend to be similar. For example, studies show that the affective reactions of native West Africans to Western (European) music differ markedly from the reactions of persons schooled in the Western tradition. On the other hand, a general emotional correspondence between people within a given culture may be expected, though even then there are too many variables to be able to predict with perfect accuracy the precise emotional response that a certain composition will elicit. After all, music does not have one unambiguous and specific emotional (or any other) meaning. However, the fact that music is not emotionally precise and narrowly predictable does not imply that it is emotionally deficient. On the contrary, music can engender responses of a variety of emotional colors, depths, and intensities. It is precisely its subjectivity, its ability to speak individually, that is its strength. The feeling side of music is real, though it is nebulous, unpredictable, ethereal, ambiguous, and mystical. Music is emotional, but emotional in a musical way. Emotion is primary in the sense that it always accompanies music, but secondary in that it is variable and mutable.

I have stated that religion and music each has an intellectual and an emotional side. Both contribute to the Christian's faith mode of living by being part of the balance needed for holistic living. In church we should expect that expressions to and from the worshiper demonstrate wholeness. Musical expression in worship must have an emotional and intellectual balance because, as we have seen, that is the nature of humans, the nature of religion, and the nature of music. At its best, music should demonstrate this life-religion-music unity in worship by a well-proportioned, reasoned, affective approach to composition.

> If there is anything that should distinguish music in church from music anywhere else, it is not so much a peculiar style, as this unity holding in perfect balance the claims of our mind and our emotions.[11]

Intellectual and Emotional Imbalances in Church Music

To emphasize emotion at the expense of reason, or reason at the expense of emotion, is to produce music that is handicapped, even crippled. "Man is not a creature moved by reason on Monday, and emotion on Tuesday, but his reason is emotional and his emotions reasonable."[12] Yet often in worship we find a lack of balance in these two areas. Such imbalance in worship expression or witness is unhealthy because only one side of human nature is participating in what should essentially be an affair of the whole person.

Church music can become imbalanced in two ways. First, the music itself may be deficient. I have said that the making of music is a matter of creative intuition and craftsmanship. Normally if music is weak it is because of poor technique rather than a lack of inspiration. However, music can be so contrived that it loses its ability to speak emotionally. Technique alone does not make good church music. For example, some critics think that music in the French Ars Nova utilized extreme complexity for complexity's sake. Johannes Galiot (second half of the fourteenth century) was "too occupied with syncopation and cross-rhythms to produce music that is moving as well as technically proficient."[13] Jacopin Selesses, in the opinion of Archibald T. Davison and Willi Apel, wrote music of such striking rhythmic complexity that it "has never been paralleled in all music history."[14] Albert Seay feels that in this historical period

> The interest already found in music as a technical toy became, by the end of the century in France, the overriding concern; we can only react, in all too many cases, with a certain amazement at the amount of sterile complexity and meaningless intricacy therein.[15]

Other examples of technically correct but emotionally barren music include study fugues written for the mastery of polyphonic compositional skill. Imogene Horsley believes such fugues to be "contrived models," which, though important as teaching devices, "should never be mistaken for musical reality."[16] James Higgs concurs:

> Probably the fugue thus made [as compositional exercise] will prove but a mechanical composition . . . the student must not mistake the means for the end, or think that, being able to analyse a composition or reproduce resemblances of its several parts or even an imitation of the whole, he is necessarily possessed of the power to produce a true and worthy work of art.[17]

Julius Portnoy notes that under certain conditions composers can create music that is "emotionally void, is highly refined, and full of technical stratagems."[18] Music requires something more than technique. To put notes down correctly, even brilliantly, but without weaving in passion, inspiration, or warmth, produces mechanistic and one-sided music. While overly intellectualized church music hardly exists in the present feeling-based cultural climate, it is nevertheless important to be aware of the possibility.

Second, an imbalance between intellect and emotion in church music may be owing to a congregation's lack of musical understanding. Hindemith shows that in order to apprehend music comprehensively the listener must have a certain amount of intellectual musical acumen. He says, however, that because individuals vary greatly in their ability to reconstruct music mentally, music should balance more and less demanding elements: that is, it should use simpler constructions (brief, symmetrical phrases, for example) and more complex constructions (such as longer, asymmetrical phrases).[19] Therefore, the level of difficulty used in the church depends upon the general musical ability of the congregation—not only the ability to perform, but also the ability to listen with understanding. Hindemith also says that the musical structure should not be so alien that one has not the faintest idea of its probable movement.[20] He is not suggesting standardized music[21] but is arguing for music that has one foot in tradition so that there can be some basis for the listener

> to conjecture with a high degree of probability its presumable course. A musical structure which due to its extreme novelty does not in the listener's mind summon up any recollections of former experiences, or which incessantly disappoints his constructive expectations, will prevent his creative cooperation.[22]

If a congregation is to experience full life in the faith, its minister of music must avoid the imbalance that either of these scenarios can engender. Music must not be so intellectual that it is emotionally barren, and it must not exceed the musical capabilities of the congregation. The minister of music must know the assembly well enough to be able to program music which members can grasp intellectually and which at the same time can serve as a stepping stone to better things. If music is trite, there is no challenge; if it is consistently too difficult, discouragement and bewilderment will set in. Intellectual listening will not take place, and the music ministry will be lopsided.

Even as the intellectual aspect of music may be stressed at the expense of emotion, so the opposite is true. The emotional aspect may be emphasized and the intellectual side ignored. For example, the gospel song is emotional through and through; Victorian hymnody and anthem literature have a strong inclination toward the cloying, sentimental, and sweet; with much late nineteenth- and early twentieth-century American church music, emotional effect is the raison d'être of the genre; and the main feature of modern religious pop-gospel-rock is the replacement of musical substance with emotional drive. Emotionalism in music employs proved patterns of sound for the manipulation of feeling—contrived, artificial, and preplanned. It is the "evocation or the seeking of emotional satisfaction divorced from reason. . . ."[23] It is the calculated short-circuiting of deep and costly experience to produce enjoyment. There is little in-depth personal involvement and wrestling with the art form. Daydreams, fantasy, and escape rather than emotional reality and maturity characterize emotionalistic music. To renounce the intellect and concentrate on the emotions is to destroy the integrity of the music. It becomes entertainment.

"Entertainment" is a prominent word in our society. We are the entertainment culture. But for the most part entertainment has yet to be accepted as viable activity in worship, at least in name. Notice the phrase "in name," for in actuality more entertainment goes on in church services than we care to admit. That is the problem—we (the music director included) do not recognize it in worship until it is too late, until a mind-set has taken hold, values and attitudes have hardened, and, lamentably, the assembly has been hooked.

To entertain (as we are using the word) is to amuse people, to wile away the time in frivolous activity, to bypass the mind, to make pleasure the end, to achieve one's goal without travail, to gratify one's need for diversion, to revert to a mindless entity where the emotions reign supreme. The predisposition toward

Dionysian enjoyment is the root of the problem. Our hedonistic society, in which pleasuring the self has become a fixation (though usually unacknowledged), has so infiltrated the church that churchgoers are often unable to differentiate between good feelings and worship. When worship services feature entertaining music (i.e., music that shortchanges the intellect) year after year, an association is established, as in Pavlov's experiments in conditioning. Then, given only the entertainment stimulus, one "worships"; no stimulus, no worship.

The problem with entertainment music is that it makes worshipers more and more self-centered, which is to say more infantile, more selfish, and more egocentric than their normal human inclination already has made them. The insatiable desire for good feelings centers worship on the self—the pleasure-seeking self. Emotionalistic self-gratification then becomes the unacknowledged purpose of worship.

Worship that is induced by and oriented toward entertainment is in fact idolatrous. The created instead of the Creator becomes the center of worship. In using emotionalistic music in worship, worshipers stimulate themselves. People feed on what they have selfishly desired and made, and in so doing whet their appetite for more of the same, in an endless cycle. The extreme subjectivity that results shows God to be a mere tool for the satisfaction of people's cravings for pleasure.

The minister of music, realizing the problems caused by music that is overintellectualized or emotionalistic, must select music very carefully. Material must not be chosen that is emotionally stacked or intellectually barren. The musician

> knows that music limited to the level of sense will result in the same satiety and eventual disgust which reward sensuality in any other area of life. He also realizes that music whose appeal is limited to the intellect will leave him and all others cold.[24]

To emphasize emotion over intellect, or intellect over emotion, is not to minister to the whole person. The life of faith demands that the music of the church both express and minister to total being. One-sidedness results in a deformed ministry and unbalanced Christians. Theologically, such art is false.

A steady diet of music that is only intellectualized, clever, astute, brilliant, and ingenious, or only escapist, amusing, cloying, entertaining, standardized, uncreative, sensational, and trite, will gradually lead worshipers to believe that the Christian faith is the same. On the other hand, balanced church music helps people develop a more mature faith, both emotionally and intellectually. The church musician has a deeper responsibility here than is commonly acknowledged. Music making can, indeed should, contribute significantly to a congregation's holistic spiritual health.

Faith Action and Tendency Gratification

The second way we are using the term "faith" is as a specific type of action. This type of faith involves stepping into the unknown as though it were known and familiar. It is "the assurance of things hoped for, the conviction of things not seen" (Heb 11:8-9 KJV). Faith cannot be reduced to calculation and logic—there is an element of the unknown about it. Yet, it is reasonable to trust its tenability. Through faith we believe we will not be poisoned by our next meal; the alarm clock has awakened us before and will (we hope!) do so again. We do not "know" these things. The evidence, however, suggests that it is reasonable to eat as though we will not be poisoned and sleep as though we will be awakened. There is a paradox here. Christianity is not sheer logic, yet it tallies with experience. The most fundamental religious paradox is that of faith and reason. To have faith there must be reason, and to have reason there must be faith.

The general Christian faith discussed in the first section (faith as a mode of being) now calls for a specific, positive, active faith. Active faith involves risk by venturing into the unknown, confident that it is reasonable to do so. Though one cannot see the end, or know the answer, one is to live creatively in freedom. To know the ending before beginning, to have the answer before asking, to know the outcome before trying, is to be safe, secure, inhibited, and ultimately bound. But the unknown should be within the normal state of existence for the believer. The Christian does not have to play it safe. Life in Christ is a risky adventure that leads home.

Church music as an expression of the Christian faith must align itself with that faith. I have said that active faith entails risk. Such an attitude can be incorporated into the music of the church in two ways. First, faith action can be shown in worship through the use of music that is somewhat difficult for the assembly to comprehend. It is risky to express the faith through the unknown because doing so requires dealing musically with uncertainty, puzzlement, and ambiguity. A music program that relies heavily on what people know or limits itself to styles based on popular approval is a repudiation of the meaning of faith. What is well known eventually becomes habitual, which is to say, comfortable. The faith adventure, musically speaking, is replaced with reliance on security. But it is theologically false to represent the Christian life as "one long rest in bed."[25]

To use music as a security blanket is dangerous. If Sunday after Sunday the musical fare is security-seeking music, then the congregation will conclude, either consciously or unconsciously, that religion is relaxation and leisure. It is something "nice." One is soothed and finally anesthetized. The risk in going to the brink—which demands faith—is denied. The Christian returns to the womb.

However, if the music director chooses music and musical styles that are fairly inscrutable, the congregation should interpret that music as portraying the element of the unknown in Christianity. One needs to deal with, in this case listen to, the unknown by welcoming its strangeness, realizing that not everything in life is within the Christian's control or immediate apprehension. In exercising faith through the faith action of creative listening, one realizes that "someone" (the composer or, theologically, God) is in control and knows what is going on. Faith will keep us from rejecting the unfamiliar and the unexplored. The Christian sees and hears through the eyes and ears of faith.

The second way that faith action can be shown in worship is through the principle of delayed gratification. Heinrich Schenker's theory that musical structure may be reduced to progressively simplified levels or shapes defined by the musical goals (cadences)[26] of the composition puts the principle of delayed gratification in perspective. There is little musical worth to a composition's bare outline. It is the process of reaching the cadential goals that contributes to and determines musical value and worth. The method of inhibiting and delaying a direct and immediate "solution" to the musical "dilemma" (the need for musical resolution) gives the composition its artistic desirability. The skill of the composer is shown by the ability to creatively delay artistic consummation. Leonard Meyer points out

> (1) that a melody of a work which establishes no tendencies, if such can be imagined, will from this point of view (and others are possible) be of no value. Of course, such tendencies need not be powerful at the outset, but may be developed during the course of musical progress. (2) If the most probable goal is reached in the most immediate and direct way, given the stylistic context, the musical event taken in itself will be of little value. And (3) if the goal is never reached or if the tendencies activated become dissipated in the press of over-elaborate or irrelevant diversions, then value will tend to be minimal.[27]

Delayed gratification is a means for establishing worth in music and is an aesthetic analogue of faith action. That is to say, by faith one knows that the goal will be reached, but the route to that goal is not immediately apparent. The sovereign God has control, and believers, in blind but responsible trust, know that the detours of life refine, cleanse, purge, purify, fashion, and shape them into something more valuable in God's eyes than they would be if life were only continuous bliss. To become a beautiful vessel one must first go through the painful experience of becoming malleable clay. The end cannot be reached without the process of becoming, and it is the becoming that requires faith. Active faith requires a willingness to experience creatively what one does not know, in the certain knowledge that the individual is being led rightly to the conclusion of the matter. Musically the church can show this theological concept of acting in faith as it affirms little-known music that is mature, incorporating the musical gratification-delaying techniques characteristic of great art. The worshiper must hear with the attitude that ultimately understanding will come but be content at the moment to listen with the ear of faith.

The principle of delayed gratification, however, is anathema in contemporary culture. Our society is patterned after its opposite—the principle of immediate gratification. So pervasive is immediate gratification that it has spawned a whole series of modern day phenomena of the "do it now" species: "piano playing in ten easy lessons," "buy now, pay later," "electronics made simple," "witnessing in three easy steps," and items such as instant mashed potatoes, literary condensations, and popular music. We are caught up in the immediacy of the moment without preparation or thought for the future.

The church must do everything it can to counteract the tendency toward immediate gratification in its own life; after all, its eschatological orientation shows us that we are, in a sense, but pilgrims and sojourners who move forward to the goal of eternity with our Lord. People of faith are not concerned with finding an answer now, because they know that ultimately there will be one. Through faith they walk from one horizon to the next. The certainty of reaching it frees Christians from the compulsion to manipulate their course in order to obtain it now. The church, however, shows its naiveté, according to Herman Berlinski, when it appropriates music for worship that has immediacy as its prime characteristic (such as commercial pop). The Judeo-Christian tradition is strongly opposed to the hedonistic principles that underlie such music. Worship is the last place music of immediate gratification should be used.[28] Pop music's neatly packaged novelty, its limited musical vision, its normalization of abnormality, and its lack of discipline and mature musical development are qualities we would expect the church to avoid in its music. With regard to this genre, Meyer says that the difference between

art music and primitive music lies in speed of tendency gratification. The primitive seeks almost immediate gratification for his tendencies whether these be biological or musical. Nor can he tolerate uncertainty. And it is because distant departures from the certainty and repose of the tonic note and lengthy delays in gratification are insufferable to him that the tonal repertory of the primitive is limited, not because he can't think of other tones. It is not his mentality that is limited, it is his maturity. Note, by the way, that popular music can be distinguished from real jazz on the same basis. For while "pop" music whether of the tin-pan-alley or the Ethelbert Nevin variety makes use of a fairly large repertory of tones, it operates with such conventional clichés that gratification is almost immediate and uncertainty is minimized.[29]

Immediate gratification, then, is antithetical to great value in music because it has poor goal-inhibiting tendencies, or in our terminology, no faith action. Music of delayed gratification manifests maturity, discipline, restraint, and the faith action of believing that beyond the present uncertainty is the certainty of achieving the goal. The church needs to testify to society that all of life is more than momentary expediency.

Church music, exhibiting faith action in musical terms, knows that its goal will be reached but does not know the route. This resistance to standardized patterns of development not only determines a piece's musical worth, but also, because the resistance is an analogue of faith action, determines the music's theological worth. One ought to be constantly surprised, delighted, pained, shocked, unsettled, and wondering as the music moves steadily toward its inevitable final cadence. If the music attempts immediate gratification through poor syntax, or banal musical material, not only will we have lesser art, but *the faith principle will be denied*. The satisfaction of the moment must be postponed so that greater depth and meaning of the whole will be advanced. We would expect that any work of art pregnant with meaning by virtue of its thoughtfully constructed internal progression would have something to say, even upon repeated hearings, and would speak loudly and clearly that, as church music, here is faith in action.

Thus we view faith action first as listening that welcomes ambiguity in church music because such listening exercises musical-theological faith. One is kept from an addiction to the secure and the comfortable. Music in its representation of the Christian life as an adventure must show adventurousness within itself. Second, faith action is shown by music that requires the listener to participate in the unfolding of the entire composition before any degree of musical fulfillment takes place. The extent to which a piece of music avoids immediately gratifying compositional devices and embraces musical ideas and compositional procedures that delay gratification, is the extent to which the piece manifests faith action. Detours in music and in life are the channels through which greater value is produced. Such action, though often unsettling, helps mature the Christian believer.

Summary and Congregational Methodology

Faith, then, is an important ingredient in living fully and well. It entails the concepts of wholeness (the life in faith) and risk (faith action), The church music program ought to reflect a walk in Christ that is mature. It should provide sustenance and edification for its constituents and be a model of the Christ-life. Such a program improves worship music by doing away with sacred-secular categories, by affirming the importance of appropriate style and compositional goodness, and by utilizing music with a balanced emotional and intellectual content. Moreover, by omitting security-seeking music, the program demonstrates that the deliberate developmental process of delayed musical gratification gives church music its value and is a musical analogue of faith. Any music that seeks to focus on the whole person emotionally and intellectually, that causes anguish as well as joy, and that does not judge its success on the basis of immediate gratification is the music that the Christian church must embrace. It is a music that witnesses to our faith and exercises our faith.

Much of what has been discussed in the preceding pages needs to be explained to a congregation if a new direction in church music is to have meaning. The days of the church musician as silent partner in the religious enterprise are over. Church musicians must become articulate prophets and teachers in order to confront the tangled web of conflicting worldviews and musical philosophies within our culture. Musicians must help congregations understand the full implications of their musical faith life both by direct teaching and by using music as a theological model. Such a venture can be an exciting partnership between clergy, laity, and musicians in the collective faith pilgrimage of the people of God. It need not be a chore. The oft-experienced misunderstandings between music director and people will be greatly reduced by this joint effort, in which the choice of music is carefully explained in biblical and theological terms. Only then will the creativity of God's people be unleashed openly and freely without reluctance or ill will. Such a collaboration will be full of promise and stimulating adventure.

7 *Stewardship*

Usually Christian stewardship is emphasized when there is a financial drive of some kind, perhaps for the church budget, the missions program, community outreach, the building fund, or other projects. Full stewardship, though, involves much more than money. It also involves giving all of oneself (time, abilities, and money) with the understanding that these are a trust from a loving God to be used to the fullest extent for the upbuilding of the kingdom. In effect, stewardship is God-oriented management—management of all that we are and have for the purpose of fulfilling God's plan for his creation, the church, and the individual.

Motivations for Stewardship

The motivation for that management is important, for without right motivation, people may come to rely (perhaps unconsciously) on their stewardship to "earn" standing before God. Salvation then might well be thought of as the result of good deeds rather than the gift of free grace. We find among the Reformers a stewardship that produced great works motivated not by the need to earn salvation but by the need to evidence God's free salvation. Motivations such as expectation of reward, legalism, loyalty to organizations, and humanistic concerns are unworthy because they are based on reasons that are oriented around law or self-interest rather than on God and his freely offered grace. In being redeemed, Christians know themselves to be freely responsible and accountable; they are gently wooed into fuller commitment. Our motivation for stewardship, then, rests first on what God has done in Jesus Christ and on our having taken upon ourselves his name in full commitment.

Second, our motivation rests on the fact that God is literally the creator and owner of everything. As recipients and stewards of his gifts, we are utterly dependent upon him. There is literally nothing that we can do in and of ourselves, for whatever we are or become is a grant or trust from God. Our dependence upon the things God gives us should humble us. We are debtors, and as stewards, owe everything to our Lord.

Third, though made in God's image through Christ, Christians find themselves to be unfinished, even as creation is unfinished. In our use of the gifts God has given us, we participate in the ongoing creation of ourselves and the world. We allow God to work through us as we fulfill our responsibility of being channels of his creativity. Each of us has both the ability and the duty to use our God-endowed talents in the service of Christ; each has the ability by virtue of being made in God's image and the duty by virtue of being both a human being and a Christian. We are free to sing, to dance, to think, to create, to be open to new possibilities. As creators we cannot be stereotyped in our actions or thinking. Nor can we be made exempt from our responsibility of being a channel.

> Every person has the task of releasing angels by shaping and transfiguring the raw materials that lie about him so that they become houses and machinery and pictures and bridges. How we do this—how we "build the earth," to use Teilhard de Chardin's phrase—is determined by the discovery and the use of our gifts.[1]

Fourth, our motivation rests in the fact that the Creator is love. The only fitting response to God's love is to love as he loves. This was the foundation of Luther's ethical principle. Love is more than idealized circumspection for the highest good; love is what causes you to give to your neighbor all that you have, and in loving your neighbor you love God. The love shown here is *agape* love, a self-giving love that asks for nothing in return and seeks no conquest or possession. *Agape* love "assumes an other-regarding style of expression which affirms the 'other' in his freedom, integrity, and uniqueness."[2] It is the love that God has shown to us in the gift of his only Son, the love that is the deepest reason for our being good stewards of all we have been given.

The motivation for stewardship, then, stems from the following: (1) God has redeemed us and we are his disciples; (2) we are debtors, for God is the owner and giver of all that we have; (3) we have been given the responsibility to use our gifts in God's full-orbed plan of ongoing creation; and (4) our response to God's love is the giving of our gifts in *agape* love. Stewardship does not come from our ingenuity but from Christ's power as we allow him to work in us.

Stewardship's Scope

In addition to understanding the reasons and motivations behind stewardship, we need to discover the parameters of stewardship. The view we have taken is that the spiritual and material aspects of life are a unity, and that stewardship involves all of it. Believers, as unified beings, are called to think in terms of the totality of life. Stewardly creativity is not a matter of the spiritual on the one hand or the material on the other. For the Christian, such a dichotomy is false. Theologian Karl Rahner questions:

> And why should not the workman, indeed any man who makes the world into what it ought to be, see the exercise of his creative powers as a sharing in that New Creation wrought in the life and death of Him who makes all things new?[3]

In being faithful, one gives everything to God, not only for the immediate good, but as a symbol of the deeper meaning of an obedient discipleship. The narrow sense of religion as prayer and praise is only a part of religious life and needs to be joined with the creative action of everyday living. The concept of the stewardship of life as a whole manifests itself every second of the day. Good stewardship from Monday through Saturday is as important as good stewardship on Sunday. It is this consistency that gives worship and Christian life credibility.

In the larger sense, a believer's vocation is Christianity. To put it another way, any type of employment is full-time Christian service. In daily life, toil becomes holy. Believers respond to God through their work. The glory of God is shown through a right use of the gifts he has given.

In his book, *My Job and My Faith,* Frederick K. Wentz includes twelve essays by laymen on the interrelation between their faith and their work. In summing up these essays, Dr. Wentz concludes that there are significant theological themes present in what he terms "lay theology" that are "the coherent interpretation of their life-style which laymen develop from their own experiences in gospel-world encounter."[4] Several themes are common throughout: creation—God, as Creator, has made and is making the world and is therefore active in business or wherever one works; stewardship—people participate in creation by utilizing their God-given talent; and vocation—the Christian and the "vocational" life are one.[5]

The church musician needs to participate fully in such a theology: that the Creator is continuing to create; that God calls music directors to continue creation through music making; and, that music and religion are interrelated. Yet music in the church is often relegated to a state of low creativity because it is not taken seriously as a way of glorifying the Creator. As a vocation it is seen not as a unification of religion and art, but as two separate worlds—one higher (spiritual) and one lower (musical). The Christian musician is often called upon, in the name of religion, to reject his stewardship of God's gift of music by creating music of such poor quality that it degrades the creative gift. Theology that concerns itself with "spiritual matters" as opposed to and over "worldly matters" will always treat art as a frivolous endeavor. This attitude is seen in John Ruskin's *Stones of Venice:*

> I never yet met with a Christian whose heart was thoroughly set upon the world to come, and, so far as human judgment could pronounce, perfect and right before God who cared about art at all.[6]

Such a position is all too common. In fact, the biblical norm is a life unity, for example, between religion and music. Let not the church muddy the waters by asking the musician to renounce one for the other. Authentic Christianity repudiates dualistic religiosity wherein the Christian composer is required to reject creative integrity when composing "religious" music but use the best creative integrity when composing for the "world." Such a dualism is misguided and fallacious.

Doing One's Best—Principle One

There are two important stewardship principles that the church musician must not neglect in the quest for a philosophical premise from which to work. We will investigate the parable of the Talents to discover these two interrelated principles: (1) doing one's best, and (2) the growth principle.

The parable is Jesus' most characteristic method of teaching. It is a literary form similar to the fable and taken from the familiar areas of common life. To understand properly what Jesus has to say through this literary genre, the parable must be seen as a genuine art form, and, as such, creative imagination is necessary in getting to the parable's intent. One must go beyond the apparent meaning of the words of the text to get to the implicit truth of the parable.

> For the kingdom of heaven is as a man travelling into a far country, who called his own servants, and delivered unto them his goods. And unto one he gave five talents, to another, two, and to another, one; to every man according to his several ability; and straightway took his journey. Then he that had received the five talents went and traded with the same, and made them five other talents. And likewise he that had received two, he also gained other two. But he that had received one went and digged in the earth, and hid his lord's money. After a long time the lord of those servants cometh, and reckoneth with them. (Matt 25:14-19 KJV)

The parable begins by stating that each servant was entrusted with something that belonged to the master. This is quite in line with what we have said both about creation and about stewardship. Everything is from God. Moreover, no one is without some gift. All of us have received things useful for the upbuilding of the kingdom—among them the gift of music, either as composer, performer, or listener. However, the parable refutes the idea of the equality of gifts. The stewards had nothing to say about what they received. In his own sovereign wisdom the master determined what each one should receive.

Such a realization should cause us to accept ourselves and our individual gifts. There are those with greater gifts and some with lesser ones. Whatever the gift, one must be faithful to use it. The accounting that took place was concerned with what each did with what was received. Faithfulness is the measure of God's accounting.[7]

The master commended the faithful servants because each had done his best with what had been given him. The phrase "doing one's best" is, no doubt, overworked. Most often it is used as an excuse for mediocrity or to indicate an effort that was unadmittedly halfhearted, lacking great care and concern. However, the principle of "doing one's best" is pregnant with meaning. God does not call for a specific level of achievement measured by objective analysis. Rather, the Lord is concerned that what each achieves is the ultimate of which that person is capable. This is the sole measure of God's evaluation of an individual's work. It is a sacrilege to waste potential.

God's measure of success is faithfulness. Faithful stewardship is related to the degree to which gifts are utilized. One of pastoral ministry's chief concerns is that people's spiritual and musical potential be tapped. We are called to develop and to give the best of what we have. Johann Sebastian Bach, a composer who in all his work brought his native talent to its highest possible development in the service of the church, was such a church musician. The musical talents we have received from God are not exempt from stewardship. A musician is "called" just as a "Christian teacher, minister, scholar, merchant, housewife, or anybody else . . . has been called by the Lord to specific work in line with his or her talents."[8] Musicians will answer for what has been entrusted to them. When composers (or performers or listeners) are content with poor work, yet are capable of better, they show poor stewardship. For example, the composer's

> awkward harmonization, the poorly worked-out counterpoint, the nebulous formal structure . . . are let pass. Who will know the difference? What difference does it actually make? Content with slipshod work, the composer fails to provide the honest craftsmanship which a proper stewardship of his gift of the spirit demands.[9]

People are called to give the best they have. That is all that is asked for. Though never objectively good enough for God, such is acceptable as the just fruit of the abilities received and will earn a loving and benevolent Father's "Well done, thou good and faithful servant."

Some Dangers

The parable of the Talents gives an overall perspective to the minister of music. Objective musical standards (which, unfortunately, are increasingly being disregarded by the church) must be seen in the light of the parable. Likewise, subjective standards (which in some quarters are the only standards applied to the music used in ministry) must also come under the parable's scrutiny.

The parable warns the objectivist that artistic merit is not the only evaluative criterion applicable to music in the church. A music program that maximizes the talent and resources of a congregation, whatever its objective standards might be, is superior in God's eyes to the music program that does not. "Poor" music may count for much more from a less musically competent congregation that is fulfilling its potential than "better" music does from a congregation that is slothful and could do more than it is doing. The church musician knows that what counts is not the artistic worth of the compositions performed but the worth of people's strivings.

But the parable also warns the subjectivist that good intentions are not enough. There are numerous dangers in the principle that "doing one's best" is all that counts, for it can become an excuse for sloth. People who think they are doing the best they can often are not. This is true, for example, regarding regular attendance by volunteers who staff the various choir ensembles, church school music programs, or instrumental groups. One's "best" might very well mean, "I'll come to rehearsal if I have nothing else to do." The thinking is that good stewardship is simply "being there when convenient." Obviously there is more to it than that.

Musicians must also exercise right attitudes. Singing or playing with a begrudging or half-hearted spirit is dishonoring to the Lord, negating both one's discipleship and one's stewardship. Ensemble rehearsal time is valuable and must be used prudently. No one (neither director nor members) has the right to waste it. Congregations and choirs should treat each song and anthem as though it were their last, a final gift sung from a cheerful heart as tribute to the King of kings. One does not bring to worship a "consecrated" vehicle of praise that is ill prepared. Christian stewardship of the gift of music requires enthusiasm, discipline, and dedication. It requires that the director understand people's musical abilities and expect that they will use them to their fullest. It requires the choir's full knowledge that doing their best will often entail sacrifice. "Doing one's best" is a matter of the spirit.

The expression, "I'm doing the best I can" often has a negative connotation. It may be used as an excuse for not doing more (quantitatively) or not doing better (qualitatively). From a biblical perspective, those who have done all that possibly can be done have lived up to the highest standards—standards not of people but of God. Even as the Lord allows no temptation above that with which we are able to cope, so he asks nothing of us except as he supplies the grace and ability to accomplish it. It is, as it were, a tug of war between law and grace—law on the one hand demanding certain artistic dues that are good and right based upon universal artistic principles, and grace on the other, simply asking for our all.

But more needs to be said. Daily living shows us to be creatures who seldom come up to our full capabilities. That is the irony of it. We say that God expects our best, but psychologists believe that in general, we use only about 10 to 20 percent of our natural intellectual ability. Pastors complain that people are too busy for church but have plenty of time for their own activities. The financial stewardship campaign may be struggling, but as a nation we spend more on alcohol and tobacco than on the needs of the church. If humanity errs, it is in the direction of not doing enough. We are still fallen.

When music has been prepared as well as it can be, given the allotted time and abilities, the music director must assure participants that since they have done their part as well as possible in preparation, the performance is now out of their hands. They should rejoice in the gift of using developed talents to their fullest—whatever they might be—not because of what people may think, but *because they know they have already pleased the Father.* The consecration of preparation is more important than the public presentation. It is not the crowd's reaction that counts, but the performer's standing before God, stripped of everything save an anointed stewardship.

Another great danger in the common usage of the phrase "doing one's best" is that the director of music will see "the best" as a reflection of something besides actual ability, often a reflection of some type of conditioning. In church music, the congregation's "best" is often determined by what it is exposed to. Though sincere and hardworking, if the director has poor musical standards and influences the whole congregation toward mediocrity, then the "best" the director knows will become the best it knows. Or if the director assumes a congregation is doing its best when they are only emulating what they have been handed by popular culture, for example, then its best is really someone else's "best." This problem includes a host of issues, including the particular style of music used, the difficulty level of music, or particular composers. The result is that the full potential of the assembly is never utilized or challenged, because its best is assumed to be something considerably less than it actually is. Obviously everyone is limited by the broader culture in some way, but for a congregation's musical level to be absolutely determined by the general culture or by a music director who lacks musical vision is to guarantee that biblical stewardship will be unfulfilled.

The essential point is that a minister of music ask people for their very best, taking into account their natural ability, training, and, to a certain extent, their cultural environment. To ask for more than they can give is to ask too much, but to ask too little is biblically reprehensible. The minister of music is a leader who must fulfill the broad stewardship call of God within the gospel framework.

Because of a high concern for Christian stewardship, all church musicians want their ensembles to perform well. Yet often, in volunteer situations, the end product of hours and hours of laborious rehearsal is so musically inferior in the eyes of the music director that he or she becomes tired, anxious, and tense, or even ill. Here the parable shows, however, that directors must be content with the people that God gifts the ensemble with and not complain about being "shortchanged" (e.g., we have no tenors!). In other words, professional musicians need not be ashamed of the fruit of the ensemble's labors when it has done its absolute best. Both level of difficulty and value of performance must be seen in the light of its strivings. The temptation is for the music director to use music that is too difficult for the group because others do it, or because it is good, or because people expect that it will be done. Trying to perform this music only ties everyone in knots. This is unnecessary if music ministers will (1) use music the ensemble can handle (educationally there is much to be said on this subject), and (2) be content to prepare as well as possible under the circumstances rather than place their contentedness in the group's ability to meet certain musical performance criteria. It is their best that ought to make the director of music feel fulfilled—not the artistic worth of their musical rendition.

All are stewards of God's gifts and are answerable to God for their use. The first stewardship principle is that God never requires more than people are capable of. He is just in his giving and receiving. He requires only our best.

Growth—Principle Two

The parable of the Talents indicates that growth, our second stewardship principle, is necessary for healthy biblical stewardship. The two profitable servants returned an increase to their lord. The two-talent servant brought four, and the five-talent servant brought ten. Good stewardship of life requires multiplying the abilities and materials provided by a beneficent God. He intends that we never stand still. To grow and live constantly in new discovery as we make our pilgrimage through time is part of the stewardship imperative. Maturing is both becoming aware and acting upon the fact that life in God encompasses ever more and more of life. Heinrich Bornkamm has forcefully

set forth this idea in his book *The Heart of Reformation Faith.*
Life is a journey, a process, a becoming. One is not full-grown
at birth. Luther said:

> This life is not being devout, but becoming devout, not being whole, but
> becoming whole . . . not a rest, but an exercise. We are not yet, but we
> shall be. It is not the end, but the way.[10]

Growth comes through some form of education (education
in the broadest sense). Through formal study, observation,
revelation, or experience, growth is a matter of never-ending
movement or change from one state to another.

Music, as a pervasive activity of life both without and within
the church, is not excused from right stewardship. Music is
found in all civilizations and often is more profuse and pervasive than other cultural manifestations. In the West, music is
everywhere. Even in worship we find that it takes up 30–50
percent of service time. It is logical to conclude that full
stewardship of life must include growth in music. We cannot
take musical maturation lightly, for more is at stake than music.
A church that promotes musical infantilism, soothing and pla-
cating the congregation rather than encouraging, even expect-
ing, musical growth, is ultimately at fault theologically.

One of God's gifts to us is the capacity to appreciate music.
Naturally, the gift varies from individual to individual as do
other gifts. Nonetheless, everyone usually possesses some inherent musical talent, and as stewards, we must all grow in
musical understanding and appreciation.

> Of course, the ability to appreciate a work of art is not ready made in
> most people: they have to be educated according to their capacity. But
> this is true for all intellectual activity.[11]

Musicians have a specific responsibility to the congregation
for fostering growth in the understanding of music because
without growth the music ministry will stagnate, ultimately
leading to a diminished stewardship, not only of music, but of
other areas of life as well. Perpetuating the status quo stunts
the growth of the entire music program. It then becomes a
baby-sitting device, an entertainment accessory; it keeps the

congregation forever on a diet of musical milk. Just as children who spent their entire educational careers in kindergarten would never develop their full potential, so churchgoers who tolerate only inferior worship music will not find, musically speaking, the fullness of the Christian life. Many churches have not taken seriously this matter of training for musical growth. They often educate inadequately and may even erode any musical understanding and skill acquired in high school or private lessons by equating poorer music with religion.

However, congregations can grow in musical understanding when they are carefully nourished. Growth manifests itself in deeper and more meaningful worship of God as well as in more viable Christian witness. Both director and people should feel a responsibility for promoting musical maturity. It cannot be left to the pastoral ministry alone to initiate, prepare, and then force-feed the congregation. The people of God need some degree of eagerness to learn. Particular thought needs to be given to the children's music program, because musical and poetic standards are best learned in childhood. Luther said:

> I am not of the opinion that because of the Gospel all arts should be rejected violently and vanish, as is desired by the heterodox, but I desire that all arts, particularly music, be employed in the service of Him who has given and created them. Unfortunately the world has become lax toward the real needs of its youth and has forgotten to train and educate its sons and daughters along proper lines. The welfare of our youth should be our chief concern.[12]

From a technical standpoint, then, the musical program should be built around the concept of music education. This is not to suggest that the church music program be thought of as just a music appreciation tool. A biblical philosophy of church music has a much different perspective than appreciating the artistic merits of great music for the sake of music. First, musical appreciation should be relative to a congregation's abilities, not to high artistic merit or low artistic merit. Second, as stewards who are called to cultivate and multiply God's gifts, the members of the church should be concerned with musical growth. The motivation for appreciation in the church is not music or the self, but *to better honor and glorify*

the Creator who will call for an accounting of these gifts.
Christians may appear from a distance to be aesthetes, but close
examination should reveal them to be, as Derek Kidner puts it,
athletes.[13]

Athletes develop as they perform more and more difficult
tasks related to a specific sport. Muscles are called upon to do
what they cannot yet do, and in the constant attempts new
levels of strength and dexterity are developed. Higher standards are then set, and the cycle begins anew. Musical fluff is
not a stimulant to musical growth. The congregation needs to
flex its musical muscles in order to grow, overcome the difficulties set before it, and reach a new plateau of understanding
from which the cycle can begin again.

Often, for example, church members ignore criticism of
poorer songs or pieces because long usage has created an
attachment. Often a believer's most cherished memories are of
church, especially when church has given that person's life
new meaning. The new convert or the growing child absorbs
the music within that particular context and associates it with
spiritual experience. Thus "church music in particular is sus-
ceptible to sentimental attachment or memories, leading us to
suspend taste when recollection of non-musical events is in-
voked."[14] Such psychological holds are very real and make
growth in music difficult. But one of the marks of a Christian
should be a teachable spirit. Understanding this, the body of
Christ should be willing to give better music a hearing and do
away with the dross.

Lack of both familiarity and pleasant associations, difficulty
of musical language, and absence of a firm resolve often make
artistic music, especially that of the twentieth century, trouble-
some to incorporate consistently into a church's musical life.
But as we exercise our musical capabilities by contending with
music that requires real exertion to comprehend, we become
musically athletic. For example, it is clear that

> contemporary music demands an active and often extensive effort from
> the listener. It is not easy music in any sense of the word. The passive
> listener, with dulled eardrums (a condition all too prevalent in this day
> and age), will *never* appreciate contemporary music.[15]

Contemporary church music of worth should be a common mode of musical expression. But a consistent educational program to expand a congregation's musical horizons is necessary if this type of music is to have a positive hearing. We must provide an environment in which theological insights can be demonstrated in terms of both old and *new* melodies, harmonies, and rhythms—the sounds of twentieth- and twenty-first-century creativity.

Music education in the church requires a ministry of music that possesses skill, ingenuity, openness, patience, and maturity. The saying "start where the people are" is sound. The problem is that often we stay there too long! To "start where the people are" has become, practically speaking, "stay where the people are," or even, in some churches that are under heavy pressure from popular culture, "regress from where the people are."

Growth in musical appreciation can take place in any congregation blessed with an ordered, structured, coherent, and comprehensive music education program. It may be a slow process, but it can be done.

Church Music Education

Specific details for the musical education of a congregation will depend upon the congregation's cultural background, native intelligence, church affiliation, attitude, and interest; however, there are two general ways that music education takes place. The more obvious is a frontal assault on the problem through technical training of some sort. This is a natural method for graded choir programs, including adult choirs, and music organizations such as orchestras, bands, bell choirs, recorder groups, and the like. The assembly can also receive limited training before the worship service for specific projects, such as a congregational concertato or a new hymn, chorus, or piece of service music. However, extensive technical training for the whole congregation in such a setting is impractical.

A second approach to congregational music education is to use a consistent diet of music that will tend to maximize its musical resources, yet not be so difficult as to alienate them. One need not lament a congregation's lack of formal musical training, because sometimes those who are musically unsophisticated are more open and eager to learn than those who have had technical training, but because of culture's influence are strongly disposed toward, and accepting of, commercial banality. If the congregation has an open attitude, consistent exposure to good music can raise its level of appreciation tremendously. The emphasis here is on doing rather than talking, on "active" listening rather than "passive" listening. It requires that one

> sit quietly, and with every bit of mental energy you possess concentrate entirely on the music. This will not be easy at first. In fact, listening can be just as tiring as any other mental activity.[16]

As music educator, the minister of music must recognize that valuing and liking are two different things. Valuing, which involves understanding and judgment, is more important than liking, which is affective and emotional. A church music program should never be predicated upon taste alone. Yet as mastery develops in the growth process of valuing good music, directors may rest assured that liking will ultimately follow valuing.

The concept of stewardship gives a balanced perspective to the whole music program. In some situations programming a steady diet of Bach, Byrd, Pinkham, Mozart, Victoria, Kodály, Brahms, Mendelssohn, Barber, and Vaughan Williams would not only not increase people's appreciation but actually so alienate them that new music could never receive a fair hearing. We should not feel that every church ought reach the level of Byrd and Pinkham. The church that makes use of this repertoire but stops growing musically is just as guilty of poor stewardship as the church that is smugly satisfied with John Stainer, Ira Sankey, John Peterson, Bill Gaither, or Mark Hayes. Although God does not set up arbitrary levels of achievement to rate us by, he is concerned that we do our best *and* that we show growth within the hereditary and environmental framework in which he has placed us. There is no place for static musical indulgence.

Another approach to music appreciation in church is to set up times, whether in the worship service, as a special mid-week study, or during church school, when a biblical perspective on church music can be spelled out. We should not expect that worshipers will automatically understand everything that goes on in the music of the church. Biblical teaching is as important to musical growth stewardship as to any other area of life. The only way a congregation will understand why music directors do what they do is through explanation and teaching. And if the director has good reasons, based on biblical principles, the church music program will make progress. True, one cannot force-feed a person musical appreciation, but it is a beginning for a believer to know that the music has been deeply thought about, prayed over, and tested by the Word of God. Then the congregation will begin to realize that there is more to music ministry than hitherto assumed. Let the musician become a teacher!

The church musician who works within stewardship guidelines will be in a much better position to minister to people than one who forces arbitrary standards on them. A music director's satisfaction will be in the growth of the assembly rather than in the performing of particular music. Whether a church sings chorales, nineteenth-century gospel songs, or CCM tunes, these are only bases from which to begin. In growing, the congregation witnesses to the gospel imperative of yielding a return on the investment God has made in his children.

A Contrapuntal Stewardship

It is dangerous for a philosophy of music to lean too heavily on one or the other of the two stewardship principles: (1) doing one's best, and (2) growth. On the one hand, there is the danger of complete subjectivism, in which no objective standards are ever included in the music program. The ultra-pragmatist uses only music that works, music that is successful, music that does what it is programmed to do. For these directors, that music is "the best." Pragmatists, who do not care whether the music ever comes under any objective authority, effectively wrap themselves and their ministry in a tight cocoon of subjectivity. However, to treat this "best" as a locked-in musical level is to misunderstand Christ's parable, because the second principle, growth, is overlooked.

On the other hand, an exclusive concern with objective growth produces the psychological warfare mentioned earlier. Every effort falls short; the satisfaction of a job well done cannot be attained because one can accept only absolute excellence. Music ministers become dissatisfied, disillusioned, even bitter, as high hopes and grand visions are dashed to the ground because of the realities of a congregation's, an ensemble's, or an individual's musical ability. The result might be for them to quit trying. We need objective criteria to measure musical growth in the church, but an objective standard must be a guide, not a slavemaster.

These two stewardship principles are only useful in tandem—a contrapuntal working relationship, if you will. Principle one (doing the best that you can) tends toward a subjectivity that is musically passive. But this is a necessary counterpoint for the objectivist, who is largely concerned with artistry. On the other hand, principle two (growth) leans toward an objectivity that is musically aggressive. This is a necessary counterpoint for the subjectivist, who is largely concerned with taste and the status quo.

The high calling of being a steward in the musical vineyard requires that we and our congregations (1) do the very best that we can in church music making, and (2) foster a far-reaching music education program that helps us grow as we exercise our musical talents. Music is a useful tool in God's grand design of making us be what he wants.

Our satisfaction comes as a result of believing deeply that God is concerned with the strivings of his people. Naturally there will be musical rewards. But greater is the "pastoral" reward of seeing one's musical ensembles through the eyes of a loving father—a father who cares more that his three-year-old loves him enough to make him a birthday card (resplendent in all its imperfections) than that the quality of the artwork on the card is inferior by artistic standards. It is the motivation behind the deed that defines the loving act. Pastoral musicians under the influence of these stewardship principles see a deeper meaning to music than just the notes. They know that God looks on the heart.

8   *Mystery and Awe*

G od is transcendent—the omnipotent, omniscient, omni-
present One. Though Christians have a personal relationship
with this all-powerful, all-knowing, and everywhere-present
Being, God nonetheless remains an unfathomable mystery.
God's otherness, unknowableness, hiddenness, and mystery,
and the awe that grips us when we contemplate the Holy, are
important considerations both in understanding who God is
and in forming a proper perspective of one's standing before
him. Indeed, some of the most important insights we can have
of the divine are of God's utter distinctiveness from all created
things and his absolute unknowability in that "we know nothing of Him except what He Himself has revealed to us."[1] God
is so exalted and so far beyond human comprehension that
whatever can possibly be imagined about him, he is infinitely
more. Luther suggests:

> Nothing is so small but God is still smaller,
> nothing is so large but God is still larger,
> nothing is so short but God is still shorter,
> nothing is so long but God is still longer,
> nothing is so broad but God is still broader,
> nothing is so narrow but God is still narrower.[2]

God, in fact, is totally and completely different from humankind. God is absolutely outside the scope of human existence and human understanding. God is not so much *a* mystery
as he *is* mystery. Brunner contends that the mystery here is not
similar to a riddle, because that would suggest that there may

be a solution that will explain the enigma. But there is no solution to the mystery that is God. We speak of him as people who grope, who see through a glass darkly, who have not the slightest ability to unravel God's incomprehensibility, who cannot even remotely understand Yahweh's inaccessibility and transcendency. Simply put, God is Divine Mystery.

God is not only mystery, he is holy. On an earthly level, holiness is customarily believed to be a quality of living. One is holy in reference to a divine standard. People are holy as they are holy unto God. Therefore, the quality of holiness as the term is commonly used is a derived one. But the holiness of God—Father, Son, and Holy Spirit—is not a quality or even an attribute as much as it is a definition of God. It is that elemental ground which permeates the very nature of Absolute Being. It separates the Creator from the created, the Incorruptible from the corruptible, the Pure from the impure. God alone can be truly holy. God is the Holy One.

The classic work that explores and develops this theme is Rudolf Otto's *The Idea of the Holy*.[3] His thought revolves around the numinous, the state of being experienced by contact with the *mysterium tremendum* of the Holy. This contemplation of the Holy produces a feeling of dread, of being overpowered, of dynamic activity, of being struck dumb, of being simultaneously attracted and repelled by the "awefulness" and awesomeness of God. One is shaken to the core when confronted with the eternal mystery of God's holiness. An individual cannot look upon a God who dwells in "light unapproachable" except indirectly, and is even then overcome completely, being filled with fear and trembling, wanting to run away yet being attracted—*the mysterium tremendum et fascinans*.

The mystery of God and the awe experienced in contemplating the Holy are important facets of biblical truth. Every believer needs to know them, for they help define a person's relationship not only with the Transcendent but also with other people. As Heinrich Bornkamm says: "this knowledge of the mystery of God, which is beyond us, is the deepest thing which binds us together as men, indeed, that which really makes us humans in the first place."[4] Not that we can fathom the depths of God's mystery and its meaning for us by erecting logical thought systems that enclose God in an earthly framework. All such attempts are doomed to failure. But we must try to deal with these eternal mysteries, and in trying we may discover some of the reality of God's transcendence and its effect upon the human family.

We attempt to speak of God's mystery and holiness, but we cannot understand it completely. We endeavor to communicate something about God through the medium of language, but God cannot be bound by language or anything else. Our attempts become mere stammerings because language's very precision and excellence for making propositional statements limits our efforts to really feel and know the inexplicable. The concepts of mystery and awe so far exceed the expressive capabilities of language that we are often tempted to give up in despair and avoid the whole business. But without a proper perspective of the transcendence of God, a radical immanence often results. God becomes a buddy and bosom pal to do our bidding.

Music and Mystery

The arts can help in this dilemma for they have a feeling tone and a drive that words do not possess. They can add significantly to our understanding of the truth of God, for "on the most subtle levels of religious thought words become clumsy; and we turn to the great artists."[5] That music has an important role in helping people to comprehend incomprehensible mysteries may be a surprise to many musicians, for we have normally thought theology to be a matter of words, including the words of our church music. However,

> Theology expresses itself not only in language, which is the chief medium of the professional theologian. Theology expresses itself also in the material forms which are the medium of the visual arts, including architecture, and in the audible forms which are the medium of the musician.[6]

If the pastoral ministry of music is to help the assembly know a little more of the fullness of God, it must see its musical proclamation in such a theological and prophetic light.

Music strives toward proclaiming and investigating mystery through the artistic exploration of time and tone. Whether or not an artist deliberately sets out to reveal something of the mystery and wonder of our world, all great art does so, and thereby shows something of the nature of the Creator. The spatial art of painting has more difficulty than the temporal art of music in expressing this quality of mystery because, being representational, most paintings are locked into known realities. The artist, then, must deliberately "interpret" or distort the subject in some way in order to reveal to others what the artist alone has seen. Abstract impressionism, which frees painting from precise meanings, is better equipped to deal with mystery than the nineteenth-century landscape painters, for example. Biganess Livingstone, a twentieth-century painter, was commissioned to do a major painting suggesting the theme implicit in the title of the chapel of Granwell School for Boys, "The Chapel of the Servant." She began with a literal depiction of Christ washing the feet of one of the disciples, but realizing that over the years and upon repeated viewings it would not convey the awe and mystery implicit in the theme, she did five more versions. Each version progressively moved from literalism to more abstraction and stylization until she felt she had captured the inner essence of her subject. She knew that the mystery inherent in the last variant could not be dissipated by complete or immediate apprehension. In her movement toward abstractness, her painting became less representational and more "musical."

The abstract quality of music is its strength. Music does not have the precision of language. Its meanings are more universal and intangible. The ethereal quality of tones moving fleetingly in time—heard but never touched, tasted, seen, or smelled—makes music the best suited of all the arts to deal with mystery. Music orders sounds or combinations of tones in a temporal sequence, only a fraction of which can be heard at any given instant. Music's constant moving and shifting, its never standing still long enough for leisurely examination, leaves us moved and stirred to our depths for unknown reasons. The creative use of music's ephemeral nature, then, is a large part of its ability to deal in mystery—an ability that meets one of our deep needs.

> The other arts, though highly inspirational, are not as mysterious as music; for music is something you cannot see, you can only hear it and feel its impact. I believe it was Plato who said, "Music is to the mind what air is to the body."[7]

It is possible to write music that is not equipped to explore mystery and engender awe. When it is composed in such a manner that everything is predigested and cozily comfortable, when stereotyped rhythms, melodies, and harmonies are blended into conventional banality, or when predetermined formulas or artistic gimmicks are used instead of fresh creativity, there is in the lessening of the artistic quality a lessening of its ability to explore mystery. Stock standardization is hardly mysterious.

Truth and Musical Composition

I have said that music's abstractness is one of the qualities that gives it a natural propensity for the mysterious. But it is not only isolated abstract sound (such as a chord or two) that contributes to its mysterious capability; it is rather the integrity of the art form as a whole that brings the mysterious quality of music into the realm of significant meaning. Why "significant"? Because music has many peripheral meanings (such as literary, pictorial, sensuous, and emotive meanings) which, though notable, are less important for church music. Ultimately, truth is one of the major meanings of music—"truth" not in the factual sense, or in the sense that pertains to mathematical or philosophical propositions, but in the sense of rightness—a rightness that is correlative with all that is known of God in creation.

When people are confronted by the notion that a primary subject of music's mystery is truth, questions inevitably arise. Is not truth a matter of tightly knit, absolutely irrevocable intellectual certainties, well defined, packaged, and arranged? How can an art, let alone such a mysterious and nonfactual art as music, have truth as its most basic meaning? Most people think of something as "true" if it is real; that is, it is true if there is a direct realism involved. Thus the flagpole in the schoolyard is truly a flagpole; and it is true that the sound of Johnny's practicing the piano is music. The proposition that the Boston Symphony Orchestra played Haydn's Symphony No. 88 in G Major last evening is true only if they actually played it. Another understanding of truth is coherence between a given proposition and a group of related explanations; that is, the proposition is necessary to more fully and systematically understand the whole. Therefore, a common practice period analysis of John Dyke's "Nicaea" is truer than a Franconian analysis, because the former harmonizes the musical facts of the hymn in a more logical and rational manner. Finally, there is the pragmatic theory, which holds that truth is what brings satisfaction or is useful. Because Muzak helps cows give more milk, it is in its usefulness seen as passing the test for being true.

Yet none of these views of truth is especially helpful in understanding the meaning of music as truth. They might help us to verify that there is such a thing as music, or that a certain musical performance it took place, or that a certain method of analysis explains it better than others, or that a particular music gives satisfactory results. But as for knowing music as truth, we are unenlightened.

Kierkegaard has suggested what is implicit in the Hebrew-Christian worldview; that is, it is more important to be truth than to know truth. The Greeks held that truth could be found primarily in ideas, the abstract intellectualization of other-worldly concepts; but the Hebrews saw truth as a dynamic orientation toward the God of the universe, the God of all truth, the God of wonder, order, mystery, etc. Truth is good action; doing, vigorously applied. When Jesus said, "I am the truth," not many understood. In answer to Pilate's question about his being king, Jesus answered that he came to bear witness to the truth and that those who are of the truth listen to him. Pilate's rejoinder: "What is truth?" He did not understand either. Jesus notes that people participate in truth as they are "of the truth" or belong "to the truth"; that is, truth is a quality of being, a derivative quality coming from a right relationship, in this case, to the Truth. In a similar vein, art can be true as it manifests right internal relationships created by the artist.

Truth in music, then, is a quality I have alluded to as rightness, a sense of internal configuration that brings the work to a logical and artistic fruition, the convincing working out of a beginning premise, a process of argumentation that brings one to the inevitable conclusion. This truth adheres to a God-appointed natural design at the root of temporal existence—a design that the artist must subscribe to intuitively and intellectually if what is created is to be true. Conversely, musical truth can be overlooked, shortchanged, or bypassed intentionally (through the artist's corruptibility) or unintentionally (through the artist's incompetence). It is the composer who establishes the truth of a musical work by the quality of compositional action.

Nevertheless, for our scientifically oriented culture, the question remains: What are the exact ingredients that make a work true and in what proportion must they be used? But there is no formula that, if followed as one follows a recipe, guarantees truth in art. We may only hint at it. In an art such as music, which is by nature the most mysterious of all the arts, preciseness, if it were possible, would take away its locus of being, dissolving all music into conventional patterns. There are principles, however, that can guide the composer, performer, and listener in the quest to establish and apprehend truth in music, principles that may not explain the greatness and the mystery of music but instead describe its wholesome, artistic, and right orientation. Music that is true is governed by these universal artistic principles.

Good musical conversation is contained in a time framework that marks out the perimeters or boundaries of the work. Within this stream of consciousness are musical sound events that define and give meaning to the framework. The sounds are not allowed to drift but are endowed with a specific time orientation related to the pulse or time ordering of the work. The principle here is that music needs to exhibit a flow, an overall feel for continuity, that moves progressively and irresistibly from beginning to end. Music is not designed to hammer a musical pulse into the mind; as a matter of fact the opposite is true, for rhythm means "flow," and an unrelenting "beat" may very well give the impression of immobility. The incessant forward movement found in artistic works is related to human life processes and the universal movement of time. Music mirrors and heightens temporal reality, and in this correspondence we see the music as being true. Establishing the long line—the total sweep, the gentle but irresistible pull of temporal universality—is a challenge to the best composer. Music must move.

Part of the continuity of great music (which I have described as flow) is determined by the cohesion of the work. Isolated and unrelated events are musically irrelevant. There must be a background unity that correlates all parts into a meaningful whole. Unity is an organic pull, a felt quality that permeates a composition so thoroughly that every part, no matter how small, is related. There is a wholeness demonstrated that is more than the sum of its parts—just as an individual is more than arms, legs, mind, and soul, and the church is more than the sum of its total members. Such unity is rooted in God. The Almighty is both one and three, Father, Son, and Spirit. That which God has made exhibits a similar wholeness. For example, every single cell of a person carries within itself the genetic coding for an entire person. This "organic unity" is also a mark of all great art. Coherence is a mark of truth.

Within this unity every composition must also exhibit diversity at various levels; digressions are necessary if the music is to have movement. Nothing in the physical world is propelled forward unless there is opposition at work somewhere. A rocket channels explosive gases in the opposite direction of the intended flight path. In walking, one moves counter to the direction of the force applied against the floor by the leg and foot. (If the foot finds no traction and continues in the direction of the push, we slip and perhaps stumble and fall.) In fine art there must be an analogue to this universal principle of opposites. Difference, contrast, tension, inequality, and diversity are important. No snowflake is exactly like another snowflake, no two trees are precisely the same, and people are not clones of an ideal human. God made the universe with such imagination that although it is one world no two things within it are exactly the same—a living, dynamic, forward-moving creation. There can be no art without the tensions of related difference, and when music attempts to operate outside the universal principles God has made—in this case the principle of variety in unity—it negates its artistic validity, becoming something inferior, perhaps even grotesque.

The craft of composition also necessitates subscribing to the principle of dominance. Some musical elements in the time frame are more important than others. The composer adopts a certain hierarchy of values in which more important features are set against the less important. Though each has a particular part to play, and therefore is important to the whole, not everything in the work is equally important. The artist is responsible not only for ensuring each musical component's individual integrity, but also for seeing that each part makes a contribution to the overall musical statement. A like principle is at work in the created order, for God set Adam and Eve over the world, the Creator being over both nature and humankind. This canon is also seen in government, church, and family life. Not everyone can be a chief, nor can every note, rhythm, or harmony be in the foreground. Music shows universal truth as it adheres to this principle of dominance.

Nevertheless, every component of a composition needs to have intrinsic worth. That is to say, it cannot be so dependent on its place in the composition for its worth that it has no value of its own. Such totally derived significance would insure that the less important elements in their supportive roles would tend to be weak and, in effect, dull. But God has given to everyone a singular standing before him—a standing whereby each person is unique, endowed with individual worth, and important enough that the Son was given for this one life as well as for the whole world. By his care of the sparrow and his numbering of the hairs on every head, we know that God cares for the individual. The uniqueness that is part of everything in the universe is an individuality given by a caring God. The artist who shows loving concern for the worth of even compositional minutiae is mirroring the way God looks at the created world. The music demonstrates truth as each part of the composition has individual worth.

We could go on describing how music manifests truth, speaking of order and freedom, tension and release, climax, balance, symmetry, economy, and other matters related to the process of creating music. The thing to note in all of this is that art in general and music in particular evidence a relationship to the universe as they participate in the universal principles found in all of existence. In a sense, art is a microcosm of the ordering of the world. As art takes upon itself the true and unchanging principles that govern natural life, it shows a rightness and truthfulness that make it worthy and that strike an unconscious chord of response within us. Not all art reaches such a high level of attainment, however, and some music violates these principles purposely for stylistic effect. The church musician in the pastoral ministry of music needs the analytical ability and intuitive feel to assign levels of value to the music used in the music program and in so doing to assess the truthfulness of a particular piece.

Music, then, in exhibiting artistic grace coming from right internal relationships, shows truth, and in being true, is akin to general revelation. Hence great art is neither unimportant nor peripheral. Those who hold that a Christian's attention should be riveted only to the Word have misunderstood Scripture. While the Bible is the final rule of faith and practice and puts knowledge into a proper framework, it never should be thought of as the sum total of all we are able to know of God. God has made us discoverers, and in the discovering we learn more of the truth. By marking us with the *imago Dei,* he has equipped us wonderfully for fulfilling the creative and cultural mandates and thereby revealing more of the truth of God. In its own right, music tells us more of the Almighty Creator. Calvin Seerveld quotes Abraham Kuyper as saying,

> Art is no fringe that is attached to the garment, and no amusement that is added to life, but a most serious power in our present existence. Art reveals ordinances of creation which neither science, nor politics, nor religious life, not even Biblical revelation can bring to light.[8]

Music has a task that goes far beyond the imagination of most church musicians. As a way of searching out eternal mysteries it is a vast frontier for new development.

Beyond the Explicitness of Words

Truth in the biblical record is not always crystal clear. Note the many Bible translations and versions, each of which attempts some further clarification of the "real" meaning; the thousands of books written to explain a specific passage; and the great contenders for the faith who disagree on general theological matters. Scripture is shrouded in mystery simply because (1) the subject matter, the infinite, is so far removed from the finite; and (2) the confines of language make communication of the numinous difficult. The Word of God ultimately lies beyond the word-symbols. Language is no doubt the most exact medium for the transfer of information about God. But even in Scripture itself, stated facts are sometimes left far behind and the writer breaks into poetry, story, parable, or song. Often the Scripture attempts to utter the unutterable, to speak the unspeakable, to make known vast mysteries that are beyond the scope of words. Language's capacity for precision does not guarantee that the true reality behind the words will be made known. Here music can help (1) by virtue of its inherently mysterious quality; (2) by its ability to explore the basic dynamics of life; and (3) by its ability to explore musically the truth of a given subject matter.

First, music's natural ambiguity and abstractness give it a quality of mystery. The mystery of the work transcends analysis and explanation because art has a life of its own, and life does not easily give up its secrets. The dissections, ponderings, and investigations to which a musical composition might be subjected reveal much about the piece. They are helpful to us. But when it comes right down to saying what makes great music artistically alive and vital, we must confess that we do not know. And this is music's mystery. We know so much about it—creating, performing, and listening—but still that inspiration, that vision, that creative spark of genius can only be expressed in terms of music and known in terms of mystery. In our ministry music should be prized for this mysterious quality, for where the biblical record needs a feeling tone, a sense of mystery, an aliveness that the text by itself does not have, God has provided us with music.

Second, music explores the fundamental dynamics of life: tension and release, struggle and conquest, movement and stillness, sound and silence, growth and decline, affirmation and rejection, life and death, and so on.[9] People experience these dynamics in everyday life but often recognize them only vaguely. The composer takes these dynamics, these truths of life, puts them into another context, and returns them to us for our edification. In music, compositional processes reflect life processes. One only needs to hear fine music to note its struggles, its conquests, its still moments, the tensions, the climaxes, its unity and diversity. Sound in motion is life in motion. It somehow stirs us to our depths. We are moved, transported to the heavenly realm, and given new vision.

Music must therefore be heard and known as something more than mere pleasant sounds for our amusement. It must be seen as a serious attempt to know more of the truth of our world—truth that is ultimately God's.

In dealing with the categories of mystery, awe, love, acceptance, rejection, etc. we find categories that music explores through its own discipline of ordered sound. These are not linked with any particular explicit theology but are akin to an implicit musical version of general revelation. These mysterious truths are unutterable, untranslatable, wordless, and unique. It is as though the solution to some perplexing matter is suddenly revealed and we exclaim in wonder, "Of course!" only to perceive by hindsight that we never realized that there was a perplexing problem in the first place. Music, as it explores "the elements of truth which are above, beneath, around, behind, and beyond the fact,"[10] gives us a little more of the truth of God, his creation, and what it means to be in a world that is fallen but which through God's grace can be redeemed.

Third, music's ability to discover the hidden meaning of text has much applied value for the church musician. Because it is confined to word symbols, even the Scripture often profits from the intuitive help of the arts to express more fully the mysterious divine reality to which the word symbols point. The same is true with regard to the texts of songs used in music ministry. Technically, the words are not the most important element of a vocal solo or a choral piece. As Susanne Langer has put it, "Every work [of art] has its being in only one order of art;" music "ordinarily swallows words and action creating (thereby) opera, oratorio, or song."[11] What we find in the highest vocal art is that the text communicates to the listener specific facts for which the musical symbols stand. We then can follow on a deeper level the musical development of the truth that is the subject of the work. Knowing the words to "Ode to Joy," for example, gives us a more definite frame of reference from which to understand what Beethoven is saying in the last movement of his Ninth Symphony. The pathos we feel in the "Crucifixus" of the J. S. Bach B Minor Mass is directed toward Christ's crucifixion because we know the text. The words, then, direct us to the specific facts, but the music itself, in its own way, goes beyond the fact. The bare words "Joyful, joyful, we adore Thee" and "He was crucified, dead and buried" do not engender in us the mystery of godly ecstasy or despair; it takes the music to bring us to knowing and feeling the truth of these facts. We can never really know how music does this—it remains a mystery. We can only give thanks that it does.

Imparting A Sense of Mystery

Both Archibald Davison and Austin Lovelace feel that one of the commonalities between music and religion is mystery. Lovelace says:

> The mind of man cannot comprehend the wonder of God; it can only see the occasional flashes of light which shine through the glory holes of life. In the awesome areas of life's mystery, music helps man to express the inexpressible.[12]

However, this is not to suggest that the worshiper automatically knows and feels the mystery of God, though at its highest and best, worship should have an overwhelming sense of the *mysterium tremendum.* In actual practice, the Christian will have to cultivate a sense of wonder in the worship of the Almighty. Printing a reminder in the Sunday bulletin or announcing from the pulpit that "The Lord is in His holy temple: let all the earth keep silence before Him" will not suffice. For

Christians to come to the full realization of the mystery and awe implicit in the worship of Almighty God, the truth of God's transcendence must be known and felt from the inside out and the outside in. Worshipers "take their shoes off"—they are on holy ground.

Perhaps remedial measures need to be implemented to restore mystery, awe, and wonder to the context for worship. Surely music cannot do it by itself, but music can help. For example, music of the popular type is made for entertainment, for immediate comprehensibility. Pop has little sense of the unknown or of mystery. It is incapable of uttering transcendent mysteries. Its style is geared toward instant and easy assimilation. To call forth awe, which Walter Nathan suggests is the ground of faith, a work of art must make demands on the hearer. Music's ability to do this depends less on literal strangeness and otherworldly associations than on its artistic value, its trueness. No matter how familiar one becomes with the Bach *St. Matthew Passion,* it never ceases to impart a sense of awe and wonder. Music of worth is the music that best helps foster mystery in worship. Herman Berlinski says:

> Why is it necessary to define the basic laws of art music in connection with the topic of this article? The definition of these basic laws [principles of time, tendency gratification, form] became necessary because these laws of art music are the laws which impart to music its transcendental value.[13]

Artistic merit is the primary consideration in finding music that can communicate the numinous.

Summary

Directors of music, as musical interpreters of the Word, find themselves face to face with the truth of God's transcendence. God is holy and the human trembles in his presence. He is "wholly other," the eternal mystery. We stand in awe of him. Such concepts presented as facts point the Christian in the direction of the deeper reality of God. However, music, in being "true" by mirroring universal artistic principles, by being creative and well-crafted, also explores and celebrates, reveals, probes, and illuminates more fully the numinous. Dry factual theological frames of reference in the context of worship can be translated by excellent music into deeply known and felt qualities. Music ministry must include music that can deal effectively with such categories. Music that is artistically stale, that does not cause the listener to utilize his intelligence and imagination, that takes an easy and (overly) familiar way, that creates the mood of perfect ease and contentment, is music that has lost its capacity to engender a sense of awe and wonder. It has lost its emotive power and its transcendental potential. Anthems and hymns that are mildly sweet, pretty, and tritely sentimental are destroyers of awe. The director of music should avoid such expressions. Music may be interesting, relevant to life, personal, knowable, and even dramatic, but it must also be artistically worthy, for with artistic grace as a foundation, music will capture and present the truth of the transcendent God. Music will be a gateway into that realm in which the worshiper will more fully grasp the truth of God's mystery and more fully experience that sense of awe that comes from a fuller realization of God's holiness. The veiled strains of the *mysterium tremendum* are in the notes.

9   *Conclusion*

The crucifixion and the resurrection are the focal points of Christianity, epochal events that have become the crossroads of history. Even as the Old Testament is centered on the exodus so the New Testament centers on the death and resurrection of our Lord. The crucifixion and resurrection are the main acts in God's self-disclosure to humankind. Without them, all other knowledge of God cannot be seen in its correct perspective.

In reality, the dying and rising of Christ are a gestalt. Separating them invalidates both. Paul declares that "Christ died for our sins according to the scriptures" (1 Cor 15:3), but he also says that "if Christ be not raised, your faith is in vain; ye are yet in your sins" (1 Cor 15:17). Only together can they be said to complete the redemptive initiative taken by God, though, as in any other larger truth, breaking it down into smaller units aids in our understanding and edification. Thus we shall look to the crucifixion and resurrection separately for whatever they have to say to the musician, and then, seeing the event as a totality, we will attempt to find an approach to the pastoral ministry of music.

The Crucifixion

The crucifixion marks the completion of the incarnation. Jesus was born as a human and died as a human. Though initially he lowered himself in coming to earth as a baby (the incarnation), in being crucified he ultimately sank into greater depths than any other human being had ever done; He fell into that abyss into which we deserve to fall . . . no one as a dying man anticipated Hell as He did.[1]

We see in this final humiliation of Jesus the absolute love God has for humanity, a love he showed to us by deed, a love on which ministers of music should model their own attitude toward those who are entrusted to their pastoral care. The humility demonstrated in the Christmas story is a far cry from the humility he endured in the cruelty, shame, and injustice of the cross. Likewise the musician is called to suffer as Christ suffered, to know that love which gives up everything. It is this quiet, gentle, meek, patient, long-suffering, and nonsensational example of our Lord that will carry the church musician through hours of discouragement and despair.

Jesus' death was the supreme sacrifice; in it he bore fully the condemnation of the human race. His great love for us is shown by his freely embracing the necessary propitiatory work upon which salvation is based. His suffering was like no other suffering; his agony a spiritual as well as a physical one. His travail in giving us new life was a travail that was redemptive, a travail instructive for all those who would affirm the Christ-life, a travail that in some mysterious way shows that suffering and discipline are not only part of the human condition but also instruments of goodness.

The artistic world is not exempt from the need for this renunciatory discipline. It is the pathway to the new. Though struggle surfaces to some degree in the art work itself, only the creator fully experiences it. As in human birth, travail accompanies the birthing of the work, the particular art object in question being, as it were, begotten rather than just made. This is not to say that all artistic endeavor has come by way of the cross—far from it. But that which breaks new ground imaginatively and with integrity comes from the hand of the master who has dealt with the discipline of crafting well, who wrestles and struggles to bring to light a vision of some shred of reality, and who does so in travail. Likewise the performer does not engage in frivolous activity, but practices and studies the music. The performer personally renounces lesser things for the necessary discipline to become a great technician and interpreter of the world's great composers. And listeners will never know the full potential of music's truth and beauty if they do not set aside the more "pleasurable" and sit at music's feet to learn (which often means frustration, a cloudy understanding that gradually clarifies as one struggles to master the unknown).

Church music, of all music, must be influenced by the cross if it is to be biblically based. Composers, performers, and congregations alike must not seek to exempt the death of our Lord from the impact it will have on their music, for the cross shows that the self-seeking pleasure syndrome inherent in the comfortable banalities of much church music is grossly in error. Both Amos Wilder and Erik Routley speak frankly about the church and its normal artistic and theological posture:

> It must be taken as a working premise that . . . no good art will be facile or easy-come-by, or borrowed or second hand. A really significant piece of art—and how much more for the church—will cost not only tuition in craft but austere spiritual discipline.[2]

> There is a danger that in the composition and practice of church music the church will always turn to what is easy and familiar, seeking to bring men to Christ by a route which by-passes the way of the cross.[3]

The cross speaks to the church musician of the need for what we have called renunciation discipline—setting aside one's ease in pursuit of the worthy and the excellent. Much Victorian church music, the gospel song, and religious rock are examples of music that omit the cross. In general, they lack the musical 'bite' to express anything but superficial notions of Christianity; there is no musical wrestling, no humble strength. The impression is one of sentimental or (in the case of rock) hysterical abandonment. While it is necessary to be under-standing of the composing, dissemination, and usage of such music without being harshly judgmental, it must be said that it plays a large part in promoting Christian infantilism, in which being a Christian means freedom from suffering, the use of God as a valet to cater to one's appetites, a certain status or accept-ability, and a comfortable niche in the world—in short, to have a God whose purpose is to serve the created. Much of this music, in being trite, repetitious, dull, strident, or musically silly, even nauseating, gives off the general aura of the comfortableness of the rocking chair, the acceptability of the popular, or the chaos of nihilism, not the discipline of the cross. The cross and one's being crucified daily with Christ, as Paul admonishes, musically requires that which does more than lull to sleep, show pop appeal, bring disorder, or appear pretty, nice, and entertaining. It requires a music of integrity that will be heard as disciplined, vigorous, even stark, requiring the listener to 'lean forward' in the pew to catch its meaning rather than sit back and be entertained. This music will require suffering and travail in its own right as it confronts the worshiper. That it does so is to know musically a little more of the reality of the cross.

The Resurrection

The resurrection as the culmination of the crucifixion is so important to the Christian religion that Emil Brunner writes:

> Without the resurrection , all discussion of the mystery of the person and saving work of Jesus Christ—indeed, all claims of the Christian faith—would be without meaning. But they have meaning because He is risen.[4]

If Jesus had remained in the grave, he could not have been the Messiah. A dead Christ is no Christ at all. He could not have been who he said he was without being the victor over sin and death. Every book of the New Testament was conceived around the resurrection and either mentions Christ's rising specifically or was written with the understanding of its being an accomplished fact. The earliest recorded sermons by the apostles give much attention to Christ's rising. These impassioned exhortations became the models for the preaching of the early church. The resurrection rallied the demoralized disciples, gave them new hope, and became the foundation of the New Testament church. Jesus' defeat of death had a markedly prominent place in their witness. The first day of every week became a celebration of the miracle of the resurrection; Sundays were Easter celebrations! They knew there could be no Christianity without the centrality of the resurrection of their Lord. It is an essential doctrine needing a new emphasis in our time not only for preaching but also for the church's music.

We see here a miracle with a depth of meaning that goes beyond the finite mind. It is the resurrection that opens to frail flesh new life, a promise for the future. It is that which breaks the bonds of the now and shows us what can be. In the resurrection we have the completion of our redemption, and in our redemption we have a whole new orientation beyond the temporal (although at the present we are still confined to the temporal). But we have a vision that gives us new imaginative insights into what is not, what could be, and what someday will be. In more direct terms, it is the resurrection that frees the human spirit to dream and that activates the imagination. Even as the cross was instructive for disciplined craftsmanship, so the resurrection is instructive for creative originality. The redeemed have opened to them a life of newness, freshness, exaltation, and creativity which should affect their entire living, including their art.

Music, which is not bound by the literally seen, tasted, smelled, or touched material of our world, is in an enviable place as far as creativity is concerned. The resurrection speaks to us of the eternal, of immortality, of timelessness, and of boundlessness. Music deals with these qualities somewhat more naturally than the other arts, for music is concerned with the ethereal, the beyond; it is truly "music of the spheres." Music is not a discipline of discovery like physics or biology; it is an investigation of that which in a sense is beyond our world yet in our world—an incarnation of sound shaped into something that attempts to transcend the world. Humankind has always been restless with the beautiful, perhaps even seeing in it a faint image of the true freedom and perfection that the Christian knows to be in Christ the risen Lord. It is the resurrection that completes redemption and opens up new vistas of intuition, of creativity, of imagination, of originality, and creative energy for every person.

It would seem, then, at first glance that we have come full circle, for we began with the doctrine of creation and its implications for creativity and now once again are back face to face with it. However, it is not that we have come full circle so much as we have followed a continuum of development. We have now a new creation and Christ, the second Adam, is the first fruit of that creation. In seeing art through the eyes of full redemption and resurrection, we must agree with Brunner, who feels that in one sense art "has more to do with Redemption than with Creation."[5] Surely this is true of good music. It brings us closer to the obscure but real feelings of the need for completion; closer to the breaking point with our world, to the casting aside of the restraints of the flesh as was done in the resurrection. Music can never do this completely, of course. But it can point to the human need for breaking free from the temporal. Whereas our study of the doctrine of creation is concerned more with the activity of this world, the resurrection is concerned more with that of the next. The resurrection opens to composers the possibility of having artistic works inspired by worlds unknown—an intuitive, imaginative plane influenced by the perfection of a new heaven and a new earth.

A certain level of artistic living is available to those who see the creative gift through the resurrection. We find in Christ's resurrection both the wellspring for creativity and a call to creativity. That is to say, in Christ, creative living is ours. Christ will give us new vision and new artistic grace. But we must feel the need to heed his call to new life (even in art), see the urgency for doing so, and know that living below the intent of the resurrected life is unnecessary poverty. It is not simply that imaging God through musical deprivation is bad (as noted in the section on the *imago Dei*). There is a more sterling need to fully appropriate the bounty of God's creative riches. That is, in the resurrection we come as close as we can to materializing life eternal. Yet we have life eternal now in our fleshly state. Therefore, as Christians we have every reason to live as close as we can to the heavenly realm—even in music. To do less is to cast away, musically speaking, the resurrection. Why live on crackers and cheese when Christ has spread before us a sumptuous banquet? Life in the resurrection of our Lord, life in the Spirit of God, is a life of limitless creative imagination—words fail us and we need to turn to music!

The crucifixion and the resurrection together open up to the Christian and to the church a whole new way of looking at life. Redemption means that the arts, in dealing with the beautiful, will have a new and special meaning for the Christian. Life in the Spirit, redeemed life, has no business with the trivial and the mediocre. Rather, a believer ought contend for richness and fullness, for that which is concerned with the right, the true, the just, and the pure. Of course there will be flexibility, which takes into consideration context conditions. We are not attempting to find one particular music for the church in the extremely narrow sense. But within the personal and churchly cultural milieu of our people we seek music that will strive toward the perfection of the resurrection. Because believers have new life, they are in the best position to realize what redemption means or should mean for the arts in general and music in particular. The church music program, because it is made up of Christians, can and should be a highly polished mirror that collects and shines forth redemption creativity, a creativity of the cross and a creativity of the resurrection, a creativity of renunciatory discipline, and a creativity of boundless imagination.

A church music program, as part of the activity of the redeemed, must clearly reflect a theistic worldview. Ideally speaking, the church is a place where God's full intentions for each person can be realized. The redemption restores to us our original place before God. Though not yet perfect, the Christian has available from God new channels through which redeemed creativity can flow. The artistic dimension of life, often estranged from the church because of many people's unwitting determination to see authenticity in the musical expression of praise and witness as unimportant, is as much a recipient of God's grace as are other areas of life. As a regenerated one, the Christian sees all of life as God's and knows that the arts belong within the community of faith because they belong to man as God's creature, because they are part of the wholeness of the life he has given us, and because in and through them we may enrich our creaturely life and praise him who is our God and King.[6]

The church music program, as a microcosm of biblical creative intentions, is the place where every member can discover, improve, and utilize the musical gift. But it is only as one understands and appreciates the theological dimensions of musical action that the true significance of that action, of that gift, comes into focus. The regenerate sing and sing well because they of all people have something to sing about. The God of the universe came, died, and rose for sinners, and that is worth more than they ever will be able to express. But Christians can give the full worth, as they know it, back to God. The assembly ascribes a worth-ship or worship to its Lord, a worship with the first fruits of its labor, a worship that is costly, a worship that stems from pure *agape* love. The musician who has a right heart cannot do less.

No matter how much we would like to assume that church music is just entertainment, just a pure neutral agent without value, or just aesthetic gratification, the crucifixion and resurrection show us otherwise. As part of *new* life, church music, in its composition, performance, and appreciation, must come by way of the cross, the way of suffering, and the way of discipline. Then the resurrection will be shown forth in joy and exultation. The music of the redeemed will be like no music on earth. It will be a music founded in the Word, a music firmly planted in the realities of this world, and reaped transformed by the boundless imagination and creativity of heaven.

A Contrapuntal Dynamic

The crucifixion and the resurrection suggest a way to make usable sense out of the varying theological ideas presented in the preceding pages, for here we see a fundamental principle common to human existence: life leads to death and death to life. A kernel of wheat dies and falls into the ground, and a new stalk arises. The essence of life lies in the cycle and tension of natural opposites: summer and winter, seedtime and harvest, night and day, movement and countermovement, negative and positive, victory and defeat, and so forth. In the theological realm, Christ lives because of the cross; we live because in Christ we have died and been reborn; the first shall be last and the last shall be first; it is only in losing one's life that it is truly found; we are justified yet sinners; it is in giving that one receives; in weakness we are strong; and on and on. The result of the death and resurrection of our Lord was, as foreordained by God, the potential redemption of everyone. But redemption as the answer to the dilemma of sin came through the balanced process of two extremes—in this case the life and death of Jesus, the greatest paradox of all. To experience new life, the old human nature must die. That is to say, there is always the crucifixion to go through to get to the resurrection. There is first the agony and then the ecstasy. We are caught between humbleness and exaltedness, imperfection and perfection. Christ's work has made believers perfect in God's eyes as far as sin goes. However, the fullness of salvation is something that must be discovered and rediscovered continually. We learn through pain, which leads to joy over and over again for the rest of our lives. The full meaning of redemption can never be fully known now. But we can and indeed must press on toward the mark of the high calling we have been given.

Full redemptive life, then, comes through the paradox of pain and joy, yes and no, freedom and discipline; musically put, a counterpoint. Church music as part of redeemed life is governed by a similar process, which is to say that church music must proceed contrapuntally.

The word counterpoint comes from the Latin *punctus contra punctum,* point counter point, or musically, note against note, melody against melody. It is used to describe music in which independent melodic lines (themes) are combined so as to affirm their dependence on one another.

A dialogue is set up between these horizontal (melodic) lines and the resulting vertical (harmonic) chords, thus shaping the particular design of the musical fabric (texture). The chordal structure, coming from the combining of the melodies, cannot be so derivative that it makes no musical sense; nor can the independent melodies themselves become totally dependent because they are governed (to a greater or lesser degree) by harmonic considerations. This process of directional balance is a type of musical argument in which "note against note" produces conversation between the horizontal and vertical aspects of music, and between the individual melodic lines. In such a contrapuntal conversation the texture shows a balance weighted in favor of the linear or horizontal emphasis—a directional balance that allows each individual line (soprano, alto, tenor, bass, and so on) its melodic independence first, and only secondarily harmonizes the line so as to produce a satisfactory succession of chords. As Walter Piston puts it, counterpoint is the "interplay of musical agreement and disagreement."[7]

In making musical decisions and judgments, the church musician must learn to weigh the relative merits of one action against the other in the light of theological propositions and counterpropositions within a given situation. Holistic maturation of the assembly's life in God takes place not through one universally circumscribed music applicable to every situation, but through a contrapuntal approach to music and theology. Church music should be based on what is known about God and what God has to say about music and about people in their various contextual conditions. We must remember the gospel admonition to balance concern for the poor with costly acts of devotion to God. A church musician's stance cannot be a hard and fast one. There will be movement and countermovement. It will be dynamic, which is to say that the music done in a particular church should reflect the counterpoint of the various and often opposite truths we have put forth.

This is a far cry from the music director's doing what people want or arbitrarily forcing "great" but unwanted music on them, or what is even more grievous, having a loose-ended variety in the music program in order to please every taste. The balance we are after is a prophetic one, a contrapuntal balance that edges people closer and closer to where they need to be in order to participate more completely in the full scope of redeemed life, including redeemed musical life. It is a balance that is directional, pointing the congregation toward a more closely aligned musical understanding with the Word, a pull toward even greater and deeper musical and theological truth.

The pastoral ministry of music is not static. It is a life pilgrimage toward a musical-spiritual maturity, a maturity that reflects God's Word in musical action—action that proceeds from the themes that have appeared many times in our investigation. Note the contrapuntal tension in the following points, which serve as a foundation to a workable philosophy of church music:

1. The church music of the redeemed must be creative. No church music should be entertaining, trite, banal, hackneyed, or stereotyped. Christians and Christian worship are less than they should be when church music is less than it should be. The creation mandate gives humans the responsibility to create well; to use only music that is excellent in musical imagination and craft. If church music does not have musical integrity, if it is uncreative and does not have musical worth, it does not belong in church.

2. The objective analysis of the worth of music is only important as it indicates that the best that can be done is being done and that growth is taking place. When choosing church music, directors must take into consideration people's abilities, cultural environment, and understanding. Strivings of people come before objective musical worth.

3. Humans are made in the image of a Creator God. They are endowed with creative talents and abilities giving them the capability of fulfilling well the creation mandate. In becoming Christians, people witness to their faith through the music they employ in church. Since church music is a musical analogy of the gospel, only that which is artistically worthy should be used.

4. Our basic posture is one of dependence, humility, and service. Our leadership is modeled after the scriptural example of the servant image culminating in Jesus.

5. The Christian faith seeks a church music that exhibits a balance between reason and emotion. Music must have good craftsmanship and exhibit a warmth that allows feeling identification with the music.

6. Church music must proceed in a manner that shows the faith action required of the Christian life. True artistic adventure in music should be seen as a musical expression of the fact that we are pilgrims walking by faith. Delayed gratification is both an aesthetic principle and a theological one. Church music

should be based upon the premise of delayed gratification if it is to be musically and theologically sound.

7. Church music should be incarnational in that the musical medium ought always be correlative to the gospel. Musical truth is important because music invariably witnesses. It is possible to negate the gospel content through poor (untruthful) form. For example, the disposition of the gospel is not inclined toward popular appeal. When the church uses pop music, the musical form gives a distorted view of the full gospel.

8. The incarnation suggests that God came to us in a form to which we could relate. Relevance is important in that there needs to be some common ground between parties. A congregation's musical profile must be taken into account in choosing music. It is imperative that there be a shared musical frame of reference between church music and the listener. A high degree of relevance is necessary for text; musical relevance operates on a less intense plane since it is not responsible for explicit propositional witness, the purview of words.

9. God's otherness, transcendence and mystery are best shown through music that exhibits high artistic integrity and is uniquely fresh, with a depth that provides the listener with ever new discoveries. On the other hand, immanence requires church music to have relevance for the listener.

The agreement and disagreement between these themes is the "point against point" upon which a beneficent theological counterpoint is based. For example, if a specific situation warrants it, we temper our legitimate concern for high creativity (point 1 above) with the contrasting concern for stewardship (point 2 above). As the congregation develops under prophetic leadership and its musical faith-walk matures, other doctrinal topics will be judiciously added. The music program will begin to reflect God's intentions for his people.

A philosophy of church music cannot be based on the theory that the purpose of a music ministry is to serve music (aesthetic approach); neither should it be based on the theory that the purpose of a music ministry is to serve people (pragmatic approach). The purpose of a coherent, comprehensive, and creative music ministry is to serve the Lord. Music becomes the full gospel in action. Then and only then will it have an authoritative prophetic word that will speak to both music and people, communicator and communicant.

The church musician's philosophy must be based on the Word of God. The theological topics we have mentioned must constantly be weighed and evaluated in the light of each other and in the context of the immediate situation. Musical methodology, based on theology, will not be static but dynamic, not harmonic but contrapuntal. The church musician will not be a musical objectivist; neither will the church musician be a musical subjectivist. Church musicians will be theological musical situationalists—they will have objective standards that are subjective in that they are situationally and theologically determined. Theological musical situationalism is the ground from which pastoral music ministry springs.

The goals and methods of the pastoral church music ministry will be dictated by a directional balance in the counterpoint of our theological formulations as they relate to each congregation. A working philosophy of church music recognizes where people are and also where they ought to be. The shape of one's musical ministry is determined by the direction in which the church needs to progress. Everything the musician does must be prophetic; that is, it must have a cutting edge that causes the congregation to discard little by little the excess baggage of poor musical-theological orientation and move toward a maturing musical expression of a maturing faith.

It is precisely this directional balance, this need to be prophetic, this motion toward a fuller musical expression and witness, that gives integrity to a ministry of music. The question is not one of present status (of what music is being used and how well it is being performed, or the degree of congregational popularity the program enjoys), but one of moving toward the mark of the ideal held up for us in Scripture. We cannot allow our congregations to become complacent, closed to anything worthwhile because of a need to satisfy the Adamic self. Yet we cannot alienate them musically. A dynamic music ministry will strive toward the highest and the best, and will do so for the right reasons. The heart will then be right before God and people.

The course charted by one's understanding of a particular congregation and by the biblical mandate to live out life creatively will not be turned aside by a tempestuous sea. Society's blitz of changing values, which often create uncertainty for the director of music, will be overcome by the musical-theological vision of what is known to be the will of God. A musician's course is set by what has been revealed concerning Yahweh's expectations for the Almighty's chosen people. Come what may, the minister of music can rest assured that it is both necessary and possible to move steadily toward the destination, even though at times one must tack against the wind.

Relying on theology rather than on aestheticism or pragmatism gives a unique perspective. We have the highest musical standards, for they come from Scripture. Yet knowing the ideal, we nevertheless strive with our people where they are. A directional balance, contrapuntally tuned to our seemingly contradictory theological themes, a balance that moves toward the musical-spiritual goal, is the framework of a workable music ministry. It is a ministry founded in the Word.

Application

To further clarify the process of using such a contrapuntal method, it would be well to include here an actual church application. I will first review in some detail the contrapuntal method, then discuss collective congregational progress, which is necessary to prophetic music ministry, and finally construct a hypothetical church situation that will demonstrate a working theological counterpoint.

I have described in Chapters 2 through 8 a number of theological topics that are the underpinnings of a biblical pastoral music ministry. In this chapter I have outlined a philosophical methodology that allows for a coherent, comprehensive, and creative use of the individual viewpoints (no matter how different) of each of these doctrinal themes. I have termed such a philosophical approach contrapuntal, for, like musical counterpoint, it is a disciplined process that allows each voice or theme its own independence and autonomy while simultaneously acknowledging the necessity of combining with the others. This theological counterpoint is the methodological design, fluid and flexible yet uncompromising in its integrity, upon which theological musical situationalism is based.

Proceeding from the paradoxical element noted in the crucifixion and resurrection of our Lord, it has seemed logical to develop for the music ministry a working counterpoint in which the "agreement" and "disagreement" of our biblical themes could be (directionally) "harmonized." Such conversation between the topics developed in these pages is the vital nerve center of the pastoral ministry of music. It is the heart of theological musical situationalism and is perhaps the most important single factor in the musical and spiritual success of music ministry.

As I have already mentioned, a working counterpoint will be dynamic, having a flexibility capable of accommodating every situation. We cannot meet the needs of a changing society by championing a music ministry that is guided in whole or in part by aesthetic or pragmatic legalistic attitudes and regulations or by pragmatic vagaries and taste whims. A multicultural, pluralistic society needs music ministry that is fluid or, in musical terminology, melodic; but at the same time modern-day congregations, pastors, music directors, singers, and instrumentalists need a philosophy that is able to impact culture without being absorbed and ultimately destroyed by it. A position capable of accommodating change but that is also capable of being disciplined by the changeless Word is necessary. I have called such an orientation contrapuntal. To the uninitiated this approach to music ministry lacks both the comfort of definitive boundaries and the intoxication of unrestrained license. At first it may seem strange and unsettling. However, the hospitable integrity found in a contrapuntal methodology based on the Word will banish any fear of the newly found freedom and discipline. It is as if we no longer are under the law but are continually in the process of discovering grace. We are freed from *having* to do this or that music either because it is "good" or because it brings "results." The music we do will depend on where the congregation is in its musical faith-walk and on the direction it needs to go to continue in that walk.

The question is routinely raised, "How realistic is it to expect musical advancement in the life of a congregation?" In a mobile society is it likely that there will be any collective musical progress? Moreover, is it realistic to expect that music ministry will be able to overcome the constant negative and destructive advance of a popularistic culture? Further, how accurately can a music director discern the collective average of a congregation's musical comprehension, or, as Routley puts it, their musical "center of gravity?"[8]

Such questions are important as well for other areas in the corporate life of the church: preaching, giving, education, missionary outreach, social concerns, evangelism. Can the people of God move forward as a group? For example, if the pastor has preached a series of sermons on tithing and over a period of months has led the assembly into a collective practice of the principle, will it be necessary to spend the next year doing the exact same thing in order to teach the 5 percent of the congregation who are new?

No matter how we answer these questions, there remains the fact that individual congregations do have collective personalities and profiles. Attend a pastor's conference and listen to the comments: such and such a church is loving, or has never reached its potential, or is a musical church, or has a real vision for missions, or is a giving church. Upon moving to a new community, ask about possible church homes and listen to the varied descriptive comments. Congregations do have collective vision, collective personality, collective spiritual tone, and a collective musical faith-walk.

Church profiles are the result of the combined characteristics of people and leaders. If parishioners were not able to bind together as the collective people of God, the church would be in disarray, with each member doing an individual "thing" off in an isolated corner. In his letters, Paul addresses the whole church so that the entire church body can progress. To the Corinthians he appeals for a unified corporate witness worthy of Jesus Christ. He asks that they join *together* "in unity of mind and thought" (1 Cor 1:10 NASB). He wants the church to have a commonality around the gospel of our Lord. In order to achieve this necessary sense of togetherness, new members need to be carefully schooled in the church's history, theology, and particular emphases. There is more to becoming a viable and contributing constituent than merely signing on the dotted line!

At the present time there is a strong move to accommodate the church to contemporary culture, to bring the church into the modern world—the real world, so to speak. Those who advocate such a stratagem usually do so on the basis that church membership is down in many denominations or to fulfill the Great Commission. True, the accommodation of the gospel is an age-old problem. But the end of the twentieth century and the beginning of the twenty-first pose special problems.[9]

Never has a Christianized culture been so fundamentally alienated from its theistic roots. The aforementioned societal worldview traits of relativism, hedonism, selfism, and materialism are the four pillars upon which present culture is based. Each of these four, which have affected every aspect of life including certain styles of music, is incompatible with the gospel message. The dilemma is clear. How does the church relate to a world so ardently opposed to the church's core beliefs?

In music, the solution to this dilemma often has been to dichotomize music from message, notes from gospel. Music, it is said, really has no worldview capability, no ability to make a statement. Music is believed to be pure neutral agent, out of the reach of theology and incapable of musical witness. Hence all music, regardless of style, is equally valid for use in church. The main criterion for use is the degree to which people like it.

The fact is that for two thousand years church music has been carefully screened. To disregard the destructive forces of our culture (relativism, hedonism, selfism, and materialism) as they affect the world of music, and to begin now to use the musical products of relativism, hedonism, selfism, and materialism is nonsensical because it undermines the central mission of the church. We are fooling ourselves if we believe a church music based in perversity will manifest biblical theism. The purpose of the church is not to reflect a people's culture. Its purpose is to reflect God. The church is not society's witness about God. It is God's witness to society. If we have to change to be that biblical witness, then so be it.

When young people join the military, they soon learn that though they retain an individual identity, they are henceforth part of a larger whole. They stand for what their unit, division, and ultimately their country stands for. As members of an organization, they take on its beliefs, policies, and methodology.

The assembly should review its presuppositions from time to time in the face of accommodative initiatives. And newcomers should be systematically taught the church's presuppositions in order that the collective faith-walk of the people will continue without having to begin over and over again. New people should see the music program as part of the developing corporate witness of a church and should make every effort to identify with what God has done in the past, is doing in the present, and will do in the future.

The church musician must use creative ingenuity in evaluating a congregation's musical and spiritual tone. Their collective musical ability and collective spiritual maturity is not always immediately apparent. Moreover, assemblies must be allowed to grow without arbitrary decisions as to how much growth is possible. The music director cannot sit back content to do the same things over and over, using the excuse that new people make such a stationary program mandatory, or, on the other hand, feel under pressure to "reach" the uninitiated with that which has the ambience and style of pop music entertainment. These practices are the opposite of prophetic ministry.

It would be a mistake to attempt to spell out exactly how the biblical themes developed in these pages always work together. They are capable of such infinite arrangement that to even hint at a standardized application would be to destroy the whole idea. There are no stock formulas to be applied mechanistically. There are only biblical principles requiring creative insights for organizing them into a meaningful working counterpoint for a particular situation.

Therefore, I will organize my often contradictory themes into a suggested design to address what might be expected in one particular hypothetical situation, realizing that every church is so unique that it is impossible to create an "average" church. I repeat, this must *not* be seen as *the* way that every music ministry will be affected by this working counterpoint. What I say about this hypothetical situation may well fit some churches, but it is not intended to be a model except in general procedure.

Writing, like melody, is linear. Music, however, has the advantage of being able to grant several melodies simultaneous existence in the same piece (hence counterpoint). Because writing deals with one sentence at a time, what follows will be a one-at-a-time written out application of each of these themes. In actual practice, however, they will be at work contrapuntally (i.e., several themes at once in beneficent balance). Some will, of course, be dominant at certain times, others at other times.

Because of the necessity of loving identification with this hypothetical congregation, I have chosen the incarnation to be the opening theme of our pastoral music ministry. The key here is that God displayed to us his care by the action of sending the Son. He did not merely talk about love; he showed us. In a ministry of music founded on biblical principles, it is no less important for the music minister to demonstrate the love of Christ. This is done by taking on the servant role modeled for us by Jesus. Becoming one with the congregation as they are served in *agape* love builds a bond of trust that is the bedrock of a prophetic music program.

The servant role is best shown through the attitude "What can I do to help?" Pastoral ministry at work here will show the music director to be an ardent under-shepherd to those in need: ministering to the sick, praying with the penitent, or teaching the novice. The musician will be a janitor when necessary or a preacher if called upon. No task is too great or too small. The director will be a "washer of feet." Jesus said it best: "If I do not wash you, you have no part with Me" (John 13:8 NASB). And again: "If I then, the Lord and the Teacher, washed your feet, you also ought to wash another's feet. For I gave you an example that you should also do as I do to you" (John 13:14–15 NASB). "Let the greatest among you become as the youngest, and the leader as one who serves" (Luke 22:26 RSV).

Even more important than doing the work of a servant is one's attitude when serving. This is no place for a proud spirit. A minister of music must serve without condescension, without malice, without resentment at having to perform tasks "beneath" a musician's "station." Paul's words clearly ring out:

> Having this attitude in yourself which was also in Christ Jesus, who, although He existed in the form of God, did not regard equality with God a thing to be grasped, but emptied Himself, taking the form of a bond-servant, and being made in the likeness of men. And being found in appearance as a man, He humbled Himself by being obedient to the point of death, even death on a cross. (Phil 2:5–8 NASB)

A love such as this is patient and kind; it does not brag and is not arrogant; it does not act unbecomingly, does not take into account a wrong suffered; love bears all things. Love never fails (see 1 Cor 13:4–8 NASB). The humility, love, and servanthood of our Lord is how we, acting for him in the ministry of music, are to conduct ourselves.

At this point our main concern in choosing music will be relevance. The music done in worship will clearly reflect the congregation's musical vocabulary. This probably means that the general style of music and even the specific repertoire will not change much. Perhaps an entire year will go by before the music director will make any substantial changes; if the tradition of the congregation is to sing with bass guitar, mandolin, tambourine and piano, it will be kept that way. On the other hand, if the pipe organ is the only accompaniment to singing, rely on it. Refrain from major changes, even in musical style. Use their music, their way of singing and playing, and their form of worship.

For ensembles, be particularly careful to avoid music that is too difficult. Keep the music on their technical level so that whatever is done is done thoroughly and well. Make time for fellowship. Use the "light touch" in rehearsal.

Time must be made in rehearsal for building a caring, ministering community. A corporate sense of God's incarnate love needs to be instilled in the group as people open up to one another and to God. Under the leadership of the director, the choir, for example, can begin to see their music as ministry to the Lord—an antiphon for the new life Christ gives. As the vertical aspect of the God-human relationship is celebrated, the horizontal aspect of the person-to-person and choir-to-congregation relationship will flourish. The edification of the assembly is the ultimate goal.

During the first year, when we are stressing these aspects of our incarnation theme, there will be opportunity to lay the groundwork necessary for the introduction of the next theme: stewardship—"doing one's best." Every church service and every rehearsal is bound to have a moment or two (the service bulletin may be the appropriate vehicle in some churches) when it would be good to mention the theological call for using well whatever God gives us. Casual remarks will go far in preparing the people for a new theme when the time comes to emphasize it.

When the director is fully confident that the incarnation theme has taken hold it is time to move to our second theme. A concept such as doing one's best is not foreign to churched people and is logical for introduction at this time. While we are developing this new theme in the music ministry of our hypothetical church, let us keep in mind that the incarnation theme continues to affect our stewardship emphasis in contrapuntal manner.

An obvious application of doing one's best is in the ensemble rehearsal. Here one is faced continually with a corporate need for practicing until excellence is reached, or until there is no more time to rehearse. The optimum performance level is set not only by the boundaries of time and musical expertise, but also by the determination to use well the gifts God has given us. To urge people to give their best time, talent, and energy in learning a piece of music is a very natural utilization of the stewardship theme.

An application of this biblical principle to the assembly might be to improve congregational singing. The majority of churches sing half-heartedly. To offer that "sacrifice of praise" (as the writer of Heb 13:15 puts it) in collective testimony requires effort. Singing requires a stewardship of one's "musical praise ability." To offer to God a musical worth-ship with sloth and indifference is disrespectful and displeasing to God. The music director can lovingly admonish the believers to a more mature posture toward congregational singing by the use of this stewardship theme. It need not be preached about, but mentioning it at an appropriate moment will help encourage them to fulfill their potential for singing well.

Other practical things such as being on time for services and rehearsals, the imperative of consistent attendance, and taking seriously the leadership role of the choir or other ensembles in worship are all fairly obvious. When there are only sixty minutes of rehearsal time, good stewardship means using them to best advantage—and that can only be done when the ensemble is there in strength for the full hour. The stewardship of good preparation will lead to effective ministry during the service.

Personnel recruitment is another area that can be helped by this stewardship principle. In giving talent, God means for it to be used. Centering on this biblical idea is a good way of enlisting people to help who have the necessary musical and spiritual qualifications. It is also a way of opening up new avenues of music ministry to people in the church who have unusual musical skills. Playing a musical saw may not be appropriate as a Sunday morning offertory, but it has the potential for demonstrating principles of musical physics to the sixth-grade choir. We use to the utmost whomever and whatever God gives us.

In working out this theme, there inevitably will come a time when the music ministry will be ready to commence with the next theme—the growth aspect of stewardship. This third theme is a very necessary corollary to "doing one's best," and is critical because it will serve as a transition to our creation theme, a theme that will be our first opportunity for strong prophetic ministry. Here we will experience what we have termed directional balance—a move toward what God intends Christians to become.

Both congregation and musical ensembles must fully understand the necessity for growth and the potential it has for leading us into new avenues of endeavor. The congregation needs to be informed of it indirectly, such as through the church newsletter (an editorial by the music director), through the Sunday bulletin, or perhaps from the pulpit. The choir or orchestra, on the other hand, may be led very carefully and systematically in rehearsal to an understanding of the biblical material on this subject.

The church's musical organizations must gain theological awareness first through teaching about growth (taking a few minutes from rehearsal or in a choir Sunday school class, etc.) and second by participating in the growth process. That is, as they rationally learn about the stewardship of growth, they must in fact experience it. Such growth might begin with the mechanistic part of musicianship: sight-singing, vocal production, phrasing, and so on. Areas need to be chosen at first in which there is real opportunity for the singers and players themselves to apprehend the progress that is being made. Once they see that it can be done, there will be less and less need for them to continually monitor their own musical advancement. It is at this point (another year, perhaps) that the level of trust in what the music director is doing will be great enough to warrant breaking some new ground.

Growth in music will inevitably bring maturing musical expressions. We say "maturing" because we never arrive at maturity. There are always new pieces of music that challenge us. But one of the reasons we want to do new music is a biblical one. We want to grow to reach the potential that God in his wisdom has given us. We want to have an increase to give to the Lord.

The question arises, "What new music?" Does the music director choose at random or on the basis of congregational taste? Obviously if we are choosing music from a biblical base rather than from an aesthetic or pragmatic one, we naturally use the doctrine that has the most to do with music making.

Remember, however, that we still have the themes of incarnation (relevance) and stewardship (doing one's best and growth) concurrent in the music ministry fabric. They will still influence what we do and how we do it.

Our fourth and fifth themes are closely related. The doctrine of creation tells us that creative music must be founded in universal artistic norms (placed by God in nature) and should break new ground with imagination and integrity. The broad *imago Dei* emphasizes that everyone has some ability to fulfill responsibly the creation and cultural mandates. Choice of music will be heavily influenced by what these doctrines say to us.

The time has come, then, for the music director to exercise the gift of discernment and choose musical pieces that can stand the scrutiny of a thorough creative (artistic) examination. Bringing into play knowledge of music theory (melody, harmony, counterpoint, form, and so on) the musician makes a judgment as to musical worth. Those pieces that clearly meet the requirements of a biblical creativity (artistry if you will) become candidates for inclusion in the repertoire. It must be taken for granted, of course, that text and difficulty level will have already been analyzed.

The personnel in the music program need to be apprised of the normality of such a creative music. It should be shown that being responsible for the creation mandate is no idle theory. Furthermore, they need to understand that creativity begins with composition, passes through performance, and ends with listening. All musical activity needs the creative spark.

Composition, however, is probably the biggest problem in establishing a creative music ministry. Often a particular style of music has, as part of its stylistic identity, an inseparable bond to noncreativity. One cannot always find creative music in one's favorite style, in which case a better alternative must be found. This is most certainly the case for pop music, which in its very essence and by definition abrogates the highest creativity for popular appeal.

Truthfully, the participants in the music program are usually not equipped to make such musical judgments. This is to be expected. But the trust built up when emphasizing the incarnation (humility, servanthood, and relevance) will give them confidence that the director has their best interest at heart. By now they will have concluded that the musician is both caring and competent. Choices will be based not on whim or personal likes but on musical value, knowledge, and intuition. Their understanding that the music minister's choices musically reflect the creatorship of God through people *(creatio continua)* will give a nobility and dignity to the process that is often missing.

Musicians, as well as the assembly as a whole, should know that musical value or creative worth is something that can be measured, even though it is not an exact science. The widespread notion that value is purely subjective is, as noted in Chapter 2, a most insidious deception. When musical value is thought to be nothing more than personal taste, biblical music ministry is impossible. It is impossible because creativity is taken out from under normal authoritative biblical norms (unity, variety, coherence, truth, imagination, and so on) and dissolved into a relativistic, even absurdist, view in which every person assigns value according to personal choice and desire. Hence it is supposedly possible for the same music to be both good and bad, creative and uncreative. These terms, which are opposites, become meaningless when they are used to describe the same thing. A worldview in which everyone does what he or she feels like produces moral, ethical, social, and artistic chaos. It is not an option for the Christian.

The contrapuntal conversation with the other three concurrent themes is bound to create a certain amount of intense discussion. It may well be that in our hypothetical church, creative music will be in tension with the actual musical vocabulary of the congregation or in tension with their preferred pop taste. A dialogue between the necessity for relevance and the necessity for creativity then ensues. What the minister of music needs to do is become a teacher so that the gap between "their" music and "creative" music, or between incarnation and creation, is lessened. Music directors must not foist their teachings on people; they must shepherd their people.

Here, then, can be seen the biblical music ministry in action. Rather than dumping a whole new set of musical rules on the church, the director carefully leads the church toward more mature musical expressions. Perhaps a few new congregational songs with good musical qualifications, for example, or some choir pieces with better artistic value, will be incorporated initially (four to six times a year) and then with increasing frequency until the church has gone as far as it can, taking into account the background, cultural environment, and education of the congregation. The themes of incarnation, stewardship, creation, and the broad *imago Dei* will provide the music minister with goals, methodological instruction, psychological satisfaction, and above all, biblical rationale.

A host of other topics inherent in the doctrine of creation and the broad *imago Dei* could be mentioned: the use of music from the past, church nurture of creativity, the use of creative gifts in Christian education, to name a few. After all, the only limit to our creativity is the boundless imagination given to us by the Creator.

In determining the specific music used for stressing creativity in our theoretical church, we may be helped by the inclusion of a sixth theme, that of faith (living life in the Christian faith). Here we see life as a unified whole—a holistic approach to life that extends to worship and to the music employed in worship. The most creative music specifically appropriate to a given church, time, and circumstance is that which will be experienced by the congregation as emotionally and intellectually balanced.

Finding such music takes thought, careful scrutiny, and patience. The congregation of which we speak needs, let us say, music from the common practice period that is emotive in design and compositionally creative. Music with an emphasis on the melodic line with rich harmonic accompaniment would be excellent. Having the intellectual side (technical craftsmanship) to consider will help keep our musical choices from being emotionalistic. Worship through such an emotionally and intellectually balanced music addresses the whole person, both in performing and in listening.

If certain congregations are able to accept more of an intellectual challenge than the church described above, music can also be found that fits them. If their practice is not to use the gift of a fine corporate musical intellect in worship, emotionalism being the norm, then the music director must teach them to open their whole selves to God. Such teaching is a prerequisite to broadening their musical horizons.

Naturally, choice of music will avoid anything that is too far ahead of the congregation. Music that sounds like gibberish, because it is much more deeply reasoned than what they are used to, will be avoided until such time as the people can begin to understand it and feel warmly toward it. This particular aspect of the faith principle helps guard against moving too far afield in one's quest for creative worship music, for worship takes place best when there is both feeling and understanding.

Ultimately a maturing ministry of music must face up to the subject of musical witness. Several new themes, each dealing with some special aspect of musical witness, will now be introduced in turn: the narrow *imago Dei,* the incarnation—form and content, and the gospel as embodied in church music.

No subject in these pages is more momentous than the seventh theme, the narrow *imago Dei.* Here we note that the church music program is a collective musical testimony of the fact that we "image" a creator. The verb "to image" takes on a special potency as we realize that in our music we show the world what we think of God. Our music speaks for us louder than our words. When banal compositions dominate the music of the church, the God we image forth is one of mediocrity, a depiction contrary to the truth. This is not to say that the church musician can ever hope to have a high enough musical image of God to actually match the Almighty's level of creativity. What we ask of our musicians is that they reflect the best creativity with which we have been endowed. We are not called to do any more than this.

As the doctrine of the *imago Dei* begins to be taken seriously and the assembly assimilates the concept, the music director will focus less on whether or not the music programmed will be accepted by the congregation and will focus more on whether or not the music reflects the creativity of

God. Responsibility for accomplishing this goal is given to every member of the music program. All music used, from solos in worship to congregational songs, from ensemble music to musical teaching materials of the children's choirs, must be chosen with the goal in mind of showing forth God's glory through musical excellence.

Another aspect of musical witness is our eighth theme, incarnation—form and content. Our concern here is that we understand that the music we do is an analogue of the gospel, that as musical expression it implicitly incarnates general gospel content, general revelation. The gospel action and the musical form will bear one another out. In being musically true, the music will bear witness to the Truth. The integrity of the gospel message found in the text of an anthem, for example, will be matched by a like integrity in the musical form.

Closely tied to form and content is our ninth theme, that of musically embodying the gospel. We are particularly concerned here that the pervasive features of pop culture be avoided in our musical expressions because these traits are so unlike the gospel. The musical embodiment of our general culture is, of course, pop music of every stripe and strain. As a musical form, pop is the musical incarnation of a post-Christian culture whose basic core values are unsupported by Christian theism. For this reason it should be avoided at this point. Instead, church music should exhibit gospel values such as honesty, goodness, creativity, and discipline. Because the gospel does not lower its standards for the sake of broad popular appeal, neither should church music. In a sense, the musical form is the show and tell of the gospel. If the form is not conformable to the intent of the message, it is misleading to use it.

The music director in our hypothetical church is going to have a difficult time persuading musicians and congregation to take musical witness seriously, particularly in this matter of gospel pop, because pop music culture is the most influential factor in the average churchgoer's musical makeup. Appreciation and understanding of musical things is formed by constant exposure to background music, recordings of secular or religious pop music, radio, and television.

As a teacher, the church musician will be faced with a real challenge here. Directors cannot succumb to a private wish to be simply people pleasers, nor can they alienate the church from pastoral music ministry by arbitrarily doing what they know they should. The counterpoint here between these witness themes and the incarnation and stewardship themes will help directors to be musically understanding, yet firm; adaptable, yet having a creative vision. It may be years before a congregation can honestly be convinced of the need to shun that which is crafted for the express purpose of achieving popularity. Perhaps some congregations will never reach this level. Yet we always try, keeping in mind the need to be prophetic.

Faith action is the tenth theme to be included in the philosophical counterpoint of our hypothetical church. Here we address the subject of tendency gratification—of seeing life as an adventurous journey complete with risks as we travel from horizon to horizon. We practice life as a faith-walk—faith being "the substance of things hoped for, the evidence of things not seen" (Heb 11:1 KJV).

We invite the choirs, instrumental groups, and congregation to join in such a musical faith-walk by the utilization of music crafted around the concept of delayed gratification. Music built upon this very basic theological and aesthetic principle is necessary at this point. Unpredictable, decidedly adventurous, ambiguous to a fault, this music will give the listener a depth to explore that will not be plumbed by repeated hearings. Such music is a description of life based on faith, a repudiation of the notion that religion is a security blanket under which nice people get comfortable.

The music director may not have as difficult a time teaching people this musical doctrine as might be expected. Living as a pilgrim is fairly common imagery, and living the life of faith is commonly believed to be a goal of every Christian. When music is translated into a representation of how we should live, there might well be an immediate identification with the intent of that music, but only if there has been sufficient teaching and explanation.

This particular subject is important to those churches that may have had a good background of creative music in only one narrow style period. The time comes when we must pull up stakes and go on. Musically, this could be the utilization of compositions based on twentieth-century harmony or a musical adventure into the sixteenth century. If we never move from a comfortable and well-entrenched, even self-satisfied position, we repudiate the faith principle.

The last theme to be woven into our contrapuntal web of themes for our hypothetical church is the transcendency of God, the *mysterium tremendum,* the mystery and awe inherent in the contemplation of the Holy, God's unknowableness and awesomeness. It takes a certain spiritual maturity to realize that we cannot own God, that we can only know of the Creator what he chooses to reveal, and that the numinous is fundamentally apart and different from human beings. One can see why this theme is necessary. In an age that stresses immanence, often a radical immanence in which God is thought of as a genie to do our bidding, the transcendency of God puts in balance the truth of the Almighty's presence and his "otherness." God is both immanent and transcendent.

The music that reinforces these ideas will, of course, be different for each congregation. For the congregation of our hypothetical church we will use a music of integrity with an emphasis on the open harmony of the early fifteenth century. Gregorian melodies also have a pathos and restrained character that lend themselves to describing transcendency musically. Certain twentieth-century styles such as that of Messiaen or Distler will also be appropriate.

Such music is exactly the opposite of the gospel-pop CCM that is so much in vogue. Stressing mystery and awe may be another tack for getting congregations and choirs to use music other than that based on immediate knowability and immediate gratification. If we try new music for biblical reasons, Christian people should make the attempt to give it a fair hearing.

Many more themes from our major topics could be developed and included in our counterpoint. But enough has been said to give us a glimmer of methodological insight as to how these topics from God's Word can help in opening up a responsible music ministry.

In weaving this contrapuntal design over a period of years, it is necessary to keep the entire design in mind when contemplating a particular decision. We must practice listening to what each has to say to us as new problems and opportunities arise from day to day. Our obligation is to stress the one that seems the most important at the time without forgetting the importance of the others.

The interplay between the separate truths of these theological themes produces the truth foundational to music ministry, a truth both accommodating and prophetic. Perhaps the best picture we have of such theological musical situationalism is God's initial invitation and subsequent plan for each of us. We see Jesus with open and everloving arms unconditionally calling all people unto himself. But after regeneration we are called to a continual life process of being conformed to the image of the Son. We come as we are, but are expected to change—caterpillars who are to evolve into butterflies, babes who are to grow into adulthood.

Pastoral music ministry should be characterized by both of these distinctions—an unconditional acceptance of people as they are and a passionate desire to teach them God's full intention for the redeemed. It is necessary that the music minister avoid the pitfalls of choosing only one side of the truth or of falsely separating the spiritual from the musical, the content from the form. If one has the correct biblical motivation and is listening to the prophetic voice of these theological themes, the director can be confident that in being a servant of the congregation he or she is ultimately the servant of God.

The key is an unquenchable and persistent vision of the marvelous contrapuntal design for music and ministry found in God's Word. Let the dynamic of this counterpoint be both rationally understood and warmly felt. Let it be the genesis for a joyful pilgrimage to new horizons.

Notes

Prologue

1. See also Calvin M. Johansson, *Discipling Music Ministry: Twenty-first Century Directions* (Peabody, Mass.: Hendrickson, 1992).

Chapter 1, Philosophical Perspectives

1. *Music in Church: Report of the Archbishop's Committee,* Noel T. Hopkins, chmn. (Westminster, S.W. I.: Church Information Office, 1960), 6.

2. Archibald T. Davison, *Protestant Church Music in America* (Boston: E. C. Schirmer, 1948), 94–142.

3. DeWitt Henry Parker, *The Principles of Aesthetics* (New York: F. S. Crofts, 1946), 297.

4. Charles T. Smith, *Music and Reason* (New York: Social Sciences, 1948), 151–52.

5. David Elton Trueblood, *Philosophy of Religion* (New York: Harper and Row, 1957), 118ff.

6. Gunnar C. Urang, *Church Music—For the Glory of God* (Moline, Ill.: Christian Service Foundation, 1956), 5.

7. W. Hines Sims, "What Is Good Church Music?" *Church Musician* 2 (1951): 12.

8. Trueblood, *Philosophy of Religion*, 41. quoting J. V. Langmead Casserly, *The Bent World* (Oxford University Press, 1955), 122.

9. Erik Routley, *The Church and Music* (London: Gerald Duckworth, 1967), 227; *Church Music and Theology* (Philadelphia: Fortress, 1965), 12ff.; Robin A. Leaver, "The Theological Character of Music in Worship," in Robin A. Leaver and James H. Litton, editors, *Duty and Delight: Routley Remembered* (Carol Stream, Ill.: Hope, 1985), 47–50.

Chapter 2, The Doctrine of Creation

1. Langdon Gilkey, *Maker of Heaven and Earth* (Anchor Books; Garden City, N.Y.: Doubleday, 1965), 4.

2. Robert Bruce McLaren, "The Threat of Aestheticism," *Christianity Today,* 7 November 1960, 16.

3. Peter A. Bertocci, "Free Will, The Creativity of God, and Order," *Current Philosophical Issues: Essays in Honor of Curt John Ducasse* (ed. Frederick C. Dommeyer; Springfield, Ill.: Charles C. Thomas, 1966), 229.

4. Gilkey, *Maker of Heaven and Earth,* 65, 120.

5. John Kobler, "Everything We Do Is Music," *Saturday Evening Post*, 19 October 1968, 46.

6. Ragnar Bring, "The Gospel of the New Creation," *Dialog* 3 (Autumn 1964): 275.

7. Cf. Leonard Verduin, *Somewhat Less Than God: The Biblical View of Man* (Grand Rapids: Wm. B. Eerdmans, 1970), 27.

8. Arthur F. Holmes, "The Idea of a Christian College," *Christianity Today,* 31 July 1970, 6.

9. Emil Brunner, *The Divine Imperative* (trans. Olive Wyon; Philadelphia: Westminster, 1947), 484.

10. W. Paul Jones, "Art as the Creator of Lived Meaning," *Journal of Bible and Religion* 31 (July 1963): 229.

11. George F. Thomas, "Central Christian Affirmations," *The Christian Answer* (ed. Henry P. Van Dusen; New York: Charles Scribner's Sons, 1945), 104.

12. Paul Waitman Hoon, *The Integrity of Worship* (New York: Abingdon, 1971), 96–97.

13. Carl Schalk, "The Shape of Church Music in the '70s," part 1, *Journal of Church Music* 13 (October 1971): 17.

14. T. S. Eliot, "The Sacred Wood," *Tradition and the Individual Talent* (6th edition; London: Methuen, 1948); quoted in James Johnson Sweeney, "The Literary Artist and the Other Arts," *Spiritual Problems in Contemporary Literature* (ed. Stanley Romaine Hopper; Harper Torchbooks/The Cloister Library; New York: Harper and Bros., 1957), 7.

15. Gordon Jacob, *The Composer and His Art* (New York: Oxford University Press, 1955), 3.

16. Edgar Wind, *Art and Anarchy* (New York: Alfred A. Knopf, 1965), 69.

17. Archie J. Bahm, "Creativity through Interdependence," *Southwestern Journal of Philosophy* 1 (Spring-Summer, 1970): 33, quoting Walter Gotshalk, *Art and the Social Order* (Chicago: University of Chicago Press, 1947), 82.

18. Wind, *Art and Anarchy,* 68.

19. Constance F. Parvey, "Christian Art in Mid-Century," *Response* 9 (Epiphany 1968): 112.

20. Herman Berlinski, "In Search of Criteria," *American Guild of Organists Quarterly* 10 (April 1965): 76.

21. Henry Grady Davis, "Worship Music in a Synthetic Culture," *Concordia Theological Monthly* 33 (December 1962): 737.

22. G. William Jones, *Sunday Night at the Movies* (Richmond, Va.: John Knox, 1968), 40.

Chapter 3, The Imago Dei

1. Edmond Jacob, *Theology of the Old Testament* (trans. Arthur W. Heathcote and Phillip J. Allcock; New York: Harper and Bros., 1958), 169–70.

2. Emil Brunner, *Dogmatics,* vol. 2, *The Christian Doctrine of Creation and Redemption* (trans. Olive Wyon; London: Lutterworth, 1952), 67.

3. Franklin Sherman, "God as Creative Artist," *Dialog* 3 (Autumn 1964): 287.

4. Dorothy L. Sayers, *The Mind of the Maker* (New York: Harcourt, Brace, Jovanovich, 1941; reprint, Westport, Conn.: Greenwood, 1970), 22.

5. Emmanuel Chapman, *Saint Augustine's Philosophy of Beauty* (New York: Sheed and Ward, 1939), 77.

6. G. C. Berkouwer, *Man: The Image of God* (Grand Rapids: Wm. B. Eerdmans, 1962), 102.

7. Joseph H. Lookstein, "How Achieve a Sacred Image of Man?," *What Is the Nature of Man?* (Religious Education Association; Philadelphia: Christian Education Press, 1959), 182.

8. Berkouwer, *Man: The Image of God,* 55.

9. W. Paul Jones, "Art as the Creator of Lived Meaning," 228.

10. Edith Schaeffer, *Hidden Art* (Wheaton, Ill.: Tyndale House, 1972), 32.

11. Ibid., 28.

12. Robert A. Cook, "That New Religious Music," *Moody Monthly,* April 1977, 40.

Chapter 4, The Incarnation

1. Parvey, "Christian Art in Mid-Century," 109.

2. Text adapted from *A Hymn of the Nativity* by Richard Crashaw in the anthem, "Summer in Winter," by Robert N. Roth (Cincinnati: Canyon, 1958).

3. F. W. Dillistone, *Dramas of Salvation* (New York: More-house-Barlow, 1967), 95.

4. The reference here is to music that glorifies brutality, violence, rape, torture, and what John Leo calls "the most hateful attitudes toward women the public culture has ever seen." Groups such as Snoop Doggy Dogg, Ice-T, Metallica, Geto Boys (who sing about cutting women's throats and slicing off their breasts), and Nine Inch Nails are immensely influential in forming the musical tastes of society. See John Leo, "The Leading Cultural Polluter," *U.S. News & World Report,* 27 March 1995, 16.

5. Calvin Seerveld, *A Christian Critique of Art and Literature* (Toronto: Association for Reformed Scientific Studies, 1968), 17.

6. Eugene L. Brand, "Congregational Song: The Popular Music of the Church," *Church Music* 1968, no. 1: 3.

7. Peter Allen, "The Problem of Communication," *English Church Music* 1966, 31.

8. Harold M. Best, *Music Through the Eyes of Faith,* Christian College Coalition (San Francisco: HarperCollins, 1993), 42.

9. Rick Warren, "On a Niche Hunt," *Leadership* 14 (Spring 1993): 23.

10. Jones, *Sunday Night at the Movies,* 48–49.

Chapter 5, The Gospel and Contemporary Culture

1. Dietrich Bonhoeffer, *The Cost of Discipleship* (New York: Macmillan, 1961), 36.

2. Ibid.

3. Denys Thompson, ed., *Discrimination and Popular Culture* (Baltimore: Penguin, 1964), 12.

4. David Willoughby, *The World of Music* (Dubuque, Iowa: Brown & Benchmark, 1996), 96–97.

5. Registered trademark of Muzak Limited Partnership.

6. Paul Hindemith, *A Composer's World* (Cambridge: Harvard University Press, 1952), 211–12.

7. Carl Halter, *God and Man in Music* (St. Louis: Concordia, 1963), 11.

8. E. Clinton Gardner, *The Church as a Prophetic Community* (Philadelphia: Westminster, 1967), 182.

9. Edwin Liehmohn, *The Chorale* (Philadelphia: Muhlenberg, 1953), 12.

10. Eric Blom, ed., *Grove's Dictionary of Music and Musicians* (5th ed.; New York: St. Martin's, 1966), 848.

11. André Hodeir, *Toward Jazz* (New York: Grove, 1962), 200.

12. Hindemith, *A Composer's World,* 126.

13. Donald Hughes, "Recorded Music," *Discrimination and Popular Culture,* 154.

14. T. W. Adorno in "On Popular Music," *Studies in Philosophy and Social Science* 9: 17, quoted in Robert William Miller, *The Christian Encounters the World of Pop Music and Jazz* (St. Louis: Concordia, 1965), 54.

15. Harry S. Broudy, "Educational Theory and the Music Curriculum," *Perspectives in Music Education* (ed. Bonnie C. Kowall; Washington, D.C.: Music Educators National Conference, 1966), 179.

16. F. J. Glendenning, *The Church and the Arts* (London: SCM, 1960), 24.

17. Routley, *Church Music and Theology,* 37.

18. Roger Hazelton, *A Theological Approach to Art* (Nashville: Abingdon, 1967), 91.

19. Arthur Korb, *How to Write Songs That Sell* (Boston: Plymouth, 1957), 8.

20. Henry Boye, *How To Make Money Selling the Songs You Write* (New York: Frederick Fell, 1970), 37.

21. Korb, *How to Write Songs That Sell,* 8.

22. Stuart Hall and Paddy Whannel, *The Popular Arts* (Boston: Beacon, 1967), 311.

23. See David Wilkerson, *The Devil's Heartbeat: Rock and Roll!* (Philipsburg, Penn.: Teen-Age Evangelism, n.d.).

24. Kurt Kaiser, "The Trends of Performance in the New Music," *The Music Journal of the Southern Baptist Church Music Conference* 5 (1973): 37.

25. Roy Harris, "Folk Songs," in *A History and Encyclopedia of Country, Western and Gospel Music* (ed. Linnell Gentry; Nashville: Clairmont, 1969), 99.

26. Routley, *Church Music and Theology,* 106.

27. Ralph Vaughn Williams, *National Music* (London: Oxford University Press, 1963), 75.

28. André Hodeir, *Jazz: Its Evolution and Essence* (trans. David Noakes; New York: Grove, 1961), 24.

29. Leonard Bernstein, *The Joy of Music* (New York: Simon and Schuster, 1959), 118.

30. Hodeir, *Toward Jazz,* 202.

31. Miller, *The Christian Encounters the World of Pop Music and Jazz,* 105.

32. Hymn by W. A. Ogden in *Popular Hymns* (n.p.: C. C. Cline, 1883), 118.

Chapter 6, Faith

1. Quoted by George Gordh in *Christian Faith and Its Cultural Expression* (Englewood Cliffs, N.J.: Prentice-Hall, 1962), 5.

2. Paul Henry Lang, "The *Patrimonium Musicae Sacrae* and the Task of Sacred Music Today," Sacred Music 93 (1966–67): 126.

3. Frank Tirro, "Choral Music," *Choral Journal* 9 (Sept.–Oct. 1967): 20.

4. John Macquarrie, "What Is the Gospel?" *Expository Times* 81 (July 1970): 299.

5. Charles R. Hoffer, *The Understanding of Music* (Belmont, Calif.: Wadsworth, 1967), 18.

6. Winfred Douglas, *Church Music in History and Practice* (New York: Charles Scribner's Sons, 1937), 8.

7. Quoted by Deryck Cooke, *The Language of Music* (London: Oxford University, 1959), 11.

8. Aaron Copland, *What to Listen for in Music* (Mentor Books; New York: McGraw-Hill, 1957), 163.

9. Smith, *Music and Reason,* 20.

10. Hoon, *The Integrity of Worship,* 212.

11. Christopher Dearnley, "The Need for a Reformed Approach to Church Music," *English Church Music* 1969, 27.

12. Paul Henry Lang, "The Musician's Point of View," *Music* 2 (December 1968): 36.

13. Denis Stevens and Alec Robertson, eds., *The Pelican History of Music,* vol. 1, *Ancient Forms to Polyphony* (Baltimore: Penguin, 1960), 284.

14. Archibald T. Davidson and Willi Apel, *Historical Anthology of Music,* vol. 1 (Cambridge: Harvard University, 1950), 220.

15. Albert Seay, *Music in the Medieval World* (Englewood Cliffs, N.J.: Prentice-Hall, 1965), 127.

16. Imogene Horsley, *Fugue: History and Practice* (New York: Free, 1966), 1.

17. James Higgs, *Fugue* (New York: H. W. Gray, n.d.), 78.

18. Julius Portnoy, *Music in the Life of Man* (New York: Holt, Rinehart and Winston, 1963), 48.

19. Hindemith, *A Composer's World,* 14–22.

20. Ibid.

21. Ibid., 126. This is a scathing attack on musical standardization.

22. Ibid., 19.

23. Erik Routley, "The Vocabulary of Church Music," *Union Seminary Quarterly Review* 18 (January 1963), 142.

24. Halter, *God and Man in Music,* 73.

25. Erik Routley, *Music Sacred and Profane* (London: Independent, 1960), 139.

26. Cadences are points of relative harmonic repose, each of which concludes the respective building blocks of a musical composition (from the smaller phrase to the larger section) and ultimately brings to an end the completed composition. The cadences of a piece are the "goals" that tonal music utilizes to establish its architectural progress.

27. Leonard Meyer, "Some Remarks on Value and Greatness in Music," *Aesthetic Inquiry: Essays on Art Criticism and the Philosophy of Art* (ed. Monroe C. Beardsley and Herbert M. Schueller; Belmont, Calif.: Dickenson, 1967), 263.

28. Herman Berlinski, "Pop, Rock and Sacred," part 2, *Music* 5 (January 1971): 48.

29. Meyer, "Some Remarks on Value and Greatness in Music," 178.

Chapter 7, Stewardship

1. Elizabeth O'Connor, *Eighth Day of Creation* (Waco, Tex.: Word, 1971), 13.

2. Alvin Porteous, *The Search for Christian Credibility* (New York: Abingdon, 1969), 172.

3. See Hoon, *The Integrity of Worship,* 186.

4. Frederick K. Wentz, "Lay Theology—A Synopsis," in *My Job and My Faith* (New York: Abingdon, 1967), 184.

5. Ibid., 186.

6. T. Glyn Thomas, "The Relationship of Art to Religion: A Study of John Ruskin," *Expository Times* 82 (March 1971), 182.

7. John S. McMullen, *Stewardship Unlimited* (Richmond, Va.: John Knox, 1966), 81.

8. H. R. Rookmaaker, "Letter to a Christian Artist," *Christianity Today,* 2 September 1966, 25.

9. Carl Schalk, "The Dilemma of the Contemporary Composer of Church Music," *Response* 7 (St. Michael and All Angels 1965): 77.

10. Heinrich Bornkamm, *The Heart of Reformation Faith* (trans. John W. Doberstein; New York: Harper and Row, 1965), 116.

11. Russell Coleburt, *The Search for Values* (New York: Sheed and Ward, 1960), 69. I would prefer to say that the ability to appreciate a work of art *fully* is not innate.

12. Taken from Walter E. Buszin, "Luther's Quotes on Music," *Journal of Church Music* 13 (October 1971): 5.

13. Derek Kidner, *The Christian and the Arts* (Chicago: Inter-Varsity, 1961), 11.

14. Robert Stone Tangeman, "Religion and the Arts," part 2, "Music and the Church," *Union Seminary Quarterly Review* 12 (March 1957): 56.

15. Arthur B. Hunkins, "The Serious Contemporary Composer and the Church Today," *Music Ministry* 2 (1970): 13.

16. Robert Elmore, "The Place of Music in Christian Life," *Christianity Today,* 31 January 1964, 8.

Chapter 8, Mystery and Awe

1. Emil Brunner, *Our Faith* (trans. John W. Rilling; New York: Charles Scribner's Sons, n.d.), 11.

2. Bornkamm, *The Heart of Reformation Faith,* 101. (The division into lines is mine).

3. Rudolf Otto, *The Idea of the Holy* (2nd Eng. ed.; trans. John W. Harvey; New York: Oxford University Press, 1958).

4. Bornkamm, *The Heart of Reformation Faith,* 102.

5. Nancy E. Sartin, "Toward a Musician's Theology," *Response* 7 (Pentecost 1965): 9.

6. Henry Grady Davis, "Theology in Relation to Arrangements for Music in the Church," *Response* 3 (Pentecost 1961): 5.

7. Van Cliburn, "Great Music a Gift from God," *Arts in Religion* 19 (Winter 1969): 3.

8. Calvin Seerveld, *A Christian Critique of Art and Literature,* 29.

9. Carl Halter has written with particular clarity on this matter of meaning, mystery, and truth in *God and Man in Music* and in "Church Music as Art and Witness," *Journal of Church Music* 5 (December 1963): 2–5.

10. Halter, "Church Music as Art and Witness," 3.

11. Quoted by Michael Tippett, "A Child of Our Time," in *The Composer's Point of View: Essays on Twentieth-Century Choral Music by Those Who Wrote It* (ed. Robert Stephan Hines; Norman: University of Oklahoma Press, 1963), 113. The brackets belong to Tippett.

12. Austin C. Lovelace and William C. Rice, *Music and Worship in the Church* (Nashville: Abingdon, 1960), 15.

13. Berlinski, "Pop, Rock and Sacred," 49.

Chapter 9, Conclusion

1. Brunner, *The Christian Doctrine of Creation and Redemption,* 363.

2. Amos Wilder, "The Arts as Interpreters of the Modern World," *Encounter* 28 (Autumn 1967): 306.

3. Routley, *Church Music and Theology,* 56.

4. J. Robert Nelson, "Emil Brunner," in *A Handbook of Christian Theologians* (ed. Dean G. Peerman and Martin E. Marty; New York: World, 1965), 416–17.

5. Brunner, *The Divine Imperative,* 500.

6. Robert W. Wood, "The Aesthetic—A Forgotten Aspect of the Christian Life," *Japan Christian Quarterly* 28 (January 1962): 36.

7. Walter Piston, *Counterpoint* (New York: W. W. Norton, 1947), 9.

8. J. Edward Moyer, "Convocation Lecture Series by Dr. Erik Routley," *News and Notes,* June 1970, 1-2, 6-8.

9. See Johansson, *Discipling Music Ministry: Twenty-first Century Directions* (Peabody, Mass.: Hendrickson, 1992).

Select Bibliography

Books

Berglund, Robert D. *A Philosophy of Church Music.* Chicago: Moody, 1985

Berkouwer, G. C. *Man: The Image of God.* Grand Rapids: Wm. B. Eerdmans, 1962.

Bernstein, Leonard. *The Joy of Music.* New York: Simon and Schuster, 1959.

Bertocci, Peter A. "Free Will, The Creativity of God, and Order." In *Current Philosophical Issues: Essays in Honor of Curt John Ducasse.* Ed. Frederick C. Dommeyer. Springfield, Ill.: Charles C. Thomas, 1966.

Best, Harold. *Music Through the Eyes of Faith.* Christian College Coalition. San Francisco: Harper/Collins, 1993.

Blom, Eric, ed. *Grove's Dictionary of Music and Musicians.* 5th ed. New York: St. Martin's, 1966.

Bonhoeffer, Dietrich. *The Cost of Discipleship.* Rev. ed. New York: Macmillan, 1961.

Bornkamm, Heinrich. *The Heart of Reformation Faith.* Trans. John W. Doberstein. New York: Harper and Row, 1965.

Boye, Henry. *How To Make Money Selling the Songs You Write.* New York: Frederick Fell, 1970.

Broudy, Harry S. "Educational Theory and the Music Curriculum." In *Perspectives in Music Education.* Ed. Bonnie C. Kowall. Washington, D.C.: Music Educators National Conference, 1966.

Brunner, Emil. *The Divine Imperative.* Trans. O. Wyon. Philadelphia: Westminster, 1947.

_____. *Dogmatics,* vol. 2, *The Christian Doctrine of Creation and Redemption.* Trans. O. Wyon. London: Lutterworth, 1952.

_____. *Our Faith.* Trans. J. W. Rilling. New York: Charles Scribner's Sons, n.d.

Chapman, Emmanuel. *Saint Augustine's Philosophy of Beauty.* New York: Sheed and Ward, 1939.

Coleburt, Russell. *The Search for Values.* New York: Sheed and Ward, 1960.

Cooke, Deryck. *The Language of Music.* London: Oxford University Press, 1959.

Copland, Aaron. *What to Listen for in Music.* Mentor Books. New York: McGraw-Hill, 1957.

Davidson, Archibald T., and Willi Apel. *Historical Anthology of Music,* 1. Cambridge: Harvard University Press, 1959.

Davison, Archibald T. *Protestant Church Music in America.* Boston: E. C. Schirmer, 1948.

Dawn, Marva. *Reaching Out Without Dumbing Down.* Grand Rapids: Eerdmans, 1995.

Day, Thomas. *Why Catholics Can't Sing: The Culture of Catholicism and the Triumph of Bad Taste.* New York: Crossroad, 1990.

Dean, Talmage W. *A Survey of Twentieth Century Protestant Church Music in America.* Nashville: Broadman, 1988.

Dillistone, F. W. *Dramas of Salvation.* New York: Morehouse-Barlow, 1967.

Doran, Carol, and Thomas H. Troeger. *Trouble at the Table: Gathering the Tribes for Worship.* Nashville: Abingdon, 1992.

Douglas, Winfred. *Church Music in History and Practice.* New York: Charles Scribner's Sons, 1937.

Faulkner, Quentin. *Choir Rehearsal Prayers.* St. Louis: MorningStar, 1990.

_____. *Wiser Than Despair: The Evolution of Ideas in the Relationship of Music and the Christian Church.* Westport, Conn.: Greenwood, 1996.

Gaebelein, Frank E. *The Christian, the Arts, and Truth: Regaining the Vision of Greatness.* Portland: Multnomah Press, 1985.

Gardner, E. Clinton. *The Church as a Prophetic Community.* Philadelphia: Westminster, 1967.

Gilkey, Langdon. *Maker of Heaven and Earth.* Anchor Books. Garden City, N.Y.: Doubleday, 1965.

Glendenning, F. J., ed. *The Church and the Arts.* London: SCM, 1960.

Gordh, George. *Christian Faith and Its Cultural Expression.* Englewood Cliffs, N.J.: Prentice-Hall, 1962.

Hall, Stuart, and Paddy Whannel. *The Popular Arts.* Boston: Beacon, 1967.

Halter, Carl. *God and Man in Music.* St. Louis: Concordia, 1963.

Harris, Roy. "Folk Songs." In *A History and Encyclopedia of Country Western and Gospel Music.* Ed. Linnell Gentry. Nashville: Clairmont, 1969.

Hazelton, Roger. *A Theological Approach to Art.* Nashville: Abingdon, 1967.

Hindemith, Paul. *A Composer's World.* Cambridge: Harvard University Press, 1952.

Higgs, James. *Fugue.* New York: H.W. Gray, n.d.

Hines, Robert Stephen, ed. *The Composer's Point of View: Essays on Twentieth-Century Choral Music by Those Who Wrote It.* Norman: University of Oklahoma Press, 1963.

Hodeir, André. *Jazz: Its Evolution and Essence.* Trans. D. Noakes. New York: Grove, 1961.

————. *Toward Jazz.* New York: Grove, 1962.

Hoffer, Charles R. *The Understanding of Music.* Belmont, Calif.: Wadsworth, 1967.

Hoon, Paul Waitman. *The Integrity of Worship.* New York: Abingdon, 1971.

Horsley, Imogene. *Fugue: History and Practice.* New York: Free, 1966.

Hughes, Donald. "Recorded Music." In *Discrimination and Popular Culture.* Ed. Denys Thompson. Baltimore: Penguin, 1964.

Hustad, Donald P. *Jubilate II: Church Music in Worship and Renewal.* Carol Stream, Ill.: Hope, 1993.

————. *True Worship: Reclaiming the Wonder and Majesty.* Carol Stream, Ill.: Hope, 1998.

Jacob, Edmond. *Theology of the Old Testament.* Trans. A. W. Heathcote and P. J. Allcock. New York: Harper and Bros., 1958.

Jacob, Gordon. *The Composer and His Art*. New York: Oxford University Press, 1955.

Johansson, Calvin M. *Discipling Music Ministry: Twenty-first Century Directions*. Peabody, Mass.: Hendrickson, 1992.

Jones, G. William. *Sunday Night at the Movies*. Richmond, Va: John Knox, 1968.

Kidner, Derek. *The Christian and the Arts*. Chicago: Inter-Varsity, 1961.

Korb, Arthur. *How to Write Songs That Sell*. Boston: Plymouth, 1957.

Leaver, Robin A. *The Theological Character of Music in Worship*. St. Louis: Concordia, 1989.

Leaver, Robin A., and James H. Litton, editors. *Duty and Delight: Routley Remembered*. Carol Stream, Ill.: Hope, 1985.

Liehmohn, Edwin. *The Chorale*. Philadelphia: Muhlenberg, 1953.

Lookstein, Joseph H. "How Achieve a Sacred Image of Man?" In *What is the Nature of Man?* Comp. Religious Education Association. Philadelphia: Christian Education, 1959.

Lovelace, Austin C., and William C. Rice. *Music and Worship in the Church*. Nashville: Abingdon, 1960.

McMullen, John S. *Stewardship Unlimited*. Richmond, Va: John Knox, 1966.

Meyer, Leonard B. "Some Remarks on Value and Greatness in Music." *Aesthetic Inquiry: Essays on Art Criticism*. Ed. Monroe C. Beardsley and Herbert M. Schueller. Belmont, Calif.: Dickenson, 1967.

Miller, Robert William. *The Christian Encounters the World of Pop Music and Jazz*. St. Louis: Concordia, 1965.

Music in Church: Report of the Archbishop's Committee, Noel T. Hopkins, chmn. Rev. ed. Westminster, S.W.I.: Church Information Office, 1960.

Myers, Kenneth A. *All God's Children and Blue Suede Shoes: Christians & Popular Culture*. Westchester, Ill.: Crossway, 1989.

Nelson, J. Robert. "Emil Brunner." *In A Handbook of Christian Theologians*. Ed. Dean G. Peerman and Martin E. Marty. New York: World, 1965.

O'Connor, Elizabeth. *Eighth Day of Creation*. Waco, Tex.: Word, 1971.

Otto, Rudolf. *The Idea of the Holy.* Trans. J. W. Harvey. Galaxy Books. 2nd Eng. ed. New York: Oxford University Press, 1958.

Parker, DeWitt Henry. *The Principles of Aesthetics.* New York: F. S. Crofts, 1946.

Pass, David B. *Music and the Church: A Theology of Church Music.* Nashville: Broadman, 1989.

Piston, Walter. *Counterpoint.* New York: W.W. Norton, 1947.

Porteous, Alvin. *The Search for Christian Credibility.* New York: Abingdon, 1969.

Portnoy, Julius. *Music in the Life of Man.* New York: Holt, Rinehart and Winston, 1963.

Routley, Erik. *The Church and Music.* London: Gerald Duckworth, 1967.

————. *Church Music and Theology.* Philadelphia: Fortress, 1965.

————. *Music Sacred and Profane.* London: Independent, 1960.

Sayers, Dorothy L. *The Mind of the Maker.* New York: Harcourt, Brace, Jovanovich, 1941. Reprint. Westport, Conn.: Greenwood, 1970.

Schaeffer, Edith. *Hidden Art.* Wheaton, Ill.: Tyndale House, 1972.

Schalk, Carl F. *Luther on Music: Paradigms of Praise.* St. Louis: Concordia, 1988.

Seay, Albert. *Music in the Medieval World.* Englewood Cliffs, N.J.: Prentice-Hall, 1965.

Seel, Thomas Allen. *A Theology of Music for Worship Derived from the Book of Revelation.* Metuchen, N.J.: Scarecrow, 1995.

Seerveld, Calvin. *A Christian Critique of Art and Literature.* Toronto: Association for Reformed Scientific Studies, 1968.

Smith, Charles T. *Music and Reason.* New York: Social Sciences, 1948.

Stevens, Denis, and Alec Robertson, eds. *The Pelican History of Music,* vol. 1, *Ancient Forms to Polyphony.* Baltimore: Penguin, 1960.

Sweeney, James Johnson. "The Literary Artist and the Other Arts." *In Spiritual Problems in Contemporary Literature.*

Ed. Stanley Romaine Hopper. Harper Torchbooks/The Cloister Library. New York: Harper and Bros., 1957.

Thomas, George F. "Central Christian Affirmations." *In The Christian Answer*. Ed. Henry P. Van Dusen. New York: Charles Scribner's Sons, 1945.

Thompson, Denys, ed. *Discrimination and Popular Culture*. Baltimore: Penguin, 1964.

Tinsley, E. J. "The Incarnation and Art." *The Church and the Arts*. Ed. F. J. Glendenning. London: SCM, 1960.

Tippett, Michael. "A Child of Our Time." *The Composer's Point of View: Essays on Twentieth-Century Choral Music by Those Who Wrote It*. Ed. Robert Stephan Hines. Norman: University of Oklahoma Press, 1963.

Trueblood, David Elton. *Philosophy of Religion*. New York: Harper and Row, 1957.

Urang, Gunnar. *Church Music—for the Glory of God*. Moline, Ill.: Christian Service Foundation, 1956.

Vaughan Williams, Ralph. *National Music*. London: Oxford University Press, 1963.

Verduin, Leonard. *Somewhat Less Than God: The Biblical View of Man*. Grand Rapids: Wm. B. Eerdmans, 1970.

Wentz, Frederick K., Ed. *My Job and My Faith*. New York: Abingdon, 1967.

Westermeyer, Paul. *The Church Musician*. Rev. ed. Minneapolis: Augsburg Fortress, 1997.

Wilkerson, David. *The Devil's Heartbeat: Rock and Roll!* Philipsburg, Penn.: Teen-Age Evangelism, n.d.

Willoughby, David. *The World of Music*. 3rd ed. Dubuque, Iowa: Brown & Benchmark, 1996.

Wind, Edgar. *Art and Anarchy*. New York: Alfred A. Knopf, 1965.

Articles

Adorno, T. W. "On Popular Music." *Studies in Philosophy and Social Science* 9: 17–23.

Allen, Peter. "The Problem of Communication." *English Church Music* (1966): 29–35.

Bahm, Archie J. "Creativity through Interdependence." *Southwestern Journal of Philosophy* 1 (Spring-Summer 1970): 29–34.

Berlinski, Herman. "In Search of Criteria." *American Guild of Organists Quarterly* 10 (April 1965): 55-59, 75-76.

_____. "Pop, Rock and Sacred," part 2. *Music* 5 (January 1971): 46-50.

Brand, Eugene L. "Congregational Song: The Popular Music of the Church." *Church Music* (1968-1): 1-10.

Bring, Ragnar. "The Gospel of the New Creation." *Dialog* 3 (Autumn 1964): 274-82.

Buszin, Walter E. "Luther's Quotes on Music." *Journal of Church Music* 13 (October 1971): 2-7.

Cliburn, Van. "Great Music a Gift from God." *Arts in Religion* 19 (Winter 1969): 3-4.

Cook, Robert A. "That New Religious Music." *Moody Monthly*, April 1977, 40.

Davis, Henry Grady. "Theology in Relation to Arrangements for Music in the Church." *Response* 3 (Pentecost 1961): 3-12.

_____. "Worship Music in a Synthetic Culture." *Concordia Theological Monthly* 33 (December 1962): 733-37.

Dearnley, Christopher. "The Need for a Reformed Approach to Church Music." *English Church Music* (1969): 23-28.

Elmore, Robert. "The Place of Music in Christian Life." *Christianity Today,* 31 January 1964, 8-9.

Halter, Carl. "Church Music as Art and Witness." *Journal of Church Music* 5 (December 1963): 2-5.

Holmes, Arthur F. "The Idea of a Christian College." *Christianity Today*, 31 July 1970, 6-8.

Hunkins, Arthur B. "The Serious Contemporary Composer and the Church Today." *Music Ministry* 2 (1970): 13-14.

Jones, W. Paul. "Art as the Creator of Lived Meaning." *Journal of Bible and Religion* 31 (July 1963): 225-32.

Kaiser, Kurt. "The Trends of Performance in the New Music." *The Music Journal of the Southern Baptist Church Music Conference* 5 (1973): 36-40.

Kobler, John. "Everything We Do Is Music." *Saturday Evening Post,* 19 October 1968, 46.

Lang, Paul Henry. "The Musician's Point of View." *Music* 2 (December 1968): 34, 36, 38-39, 60-61.

_____. "The *Patrimonium Musicae Sacrae* and the Task of Sacred Music Today." *Sacred Music* 93 (Winter 1966-67): 119-31.

McLaren, Robert Bruce. "The Threat of Aestheticism." *Christianity Today*, 7 November 1960, 16, 18.

Macquarrie, John. "What Is the Gospel?" part 1. *Expository Times* 81 (July 1970): 296–300.

Moyer, J. Edward. "Convocation Lecture Series by Dr. Erik Routley." *News and Notes* (June 1970): 1–2, 6–8.

Parvey, Constance F. "Christian Art in Mid-Century." *Response* 9 (Epiphany 1968): 107–15.

Rookmaaker, H. R. "Letter to a Christian Artist." *Christianity Today,* 2 September 1966, 25–27.

Routley, Erik. "The Vocabulary of Church Music." *Union Seminary Quarterly Review* 18 (January 1963): 135–47.

Sartin, Nancy E. "Toward a Musician's Theology." *Response* 7 (Pentecost 1965): 9–13.

Schalk, Carl. "The Dilemma of the Contemporary Composer of Church Music." *Response* 7 (St. Michael and All Angels 1965): 69–78.

————. "The Shape of Church Music in the '70s," part 1. *Journal of Church Music* 13 (October 1971): 17–20.

Sherman, Franklin. "God as Creative Artist." *Dialog* 3 (Autumn 1964): 283–87.

Sims, W. Hines. "What Is Good Church Music?" *Church Musician* 2 (November 1951): 12.

Tangeman, Robert S. "Religion and the Arts," part 2, "Music and the Church." *Union Seminary Quarterly Review* 12 (March 1957): 55–60.

Thomas, T. Glyn. "The Relationship of Art to Religion: A Study of John Ruskin." *Expository Times* 82 (March 1971): 182–85.

Tirro, Frank. "Choral Music." Choral Journal 9 (September–October 1967): 20–21.

Warren, Rick. "On a Niche Hunt." *Leadership* 14 (Spring 1993): 21–28.

Wilder, Amos N. "The Arts as Interpreters of the Modern World." *Encounter* 28 (Autumn 1967): 305–12.

Wood, Robert W. "The Aesthetic—A Forgotten Aspect of the Christian Life." *Japan Christian Quarterly* 28 (January 1962): 22–36.

Index

absolutes ix, x, 3, 6
absurdity 11, 24
abstract art and music 52, 126-27
accommodation, musical and cultural x, 50, 66-67, 152, 154-55, 168
accounting, stewardship 118
Acts 10 and 13 15
Adamic nature 72, 150. *See also* fall, the
adventure 99-100, 103, 105, 148, 166-67
advertising. *See* marketing
aesthetes 118
aesthetic principles, universal 126. *See* universal aesthetic principles
aestheticism 2-7, 42, 44, 145, 149, 151-52
aesthetics x, 3-4, 34
aesthetics, autonomous, theory of 90
aesthetics, heteronomous, theory of 90
affective life 93
African culture 93-94
agape love 43-44, 107, 139, 145, 156-57
aleatory composition 11-12
ambiguity, compositional 100-101, 103, 123-24
amoralism 14
amusement 59, 71. *See also* entertainment

analogue of the gospel, music as 25, 49, 52, 67, 69, 76, 81, 100, 103, 148-49, 150, 164-65
Ananias 58
anthropomorphism 27, 93
antinomianism (dualism) 60, 109-10
Apel, Willi 95
Apostles' Creed 8
application of theology, contrapuntal 151-68
appropriateness, musical 69, 89
Aquinas, Thomas 29
arrangements, musical 70, 73
art and theology 125-26, 133-35, 144
art as commodity 73
art music 102
artist 21, 30-31, 40, 72, 126
artistic communication 53. *See also* communication
artistic integrity 15, 72, 74, 144
artistic intelligibility 11
artistic norms 3, 47, 161
artistic vision 30, 51
artistry 42, 127, 136
arts (the) 6, 35-36, 40, 64, 126
athletes 118
attitude 89, 112-14, 117, 122, 151, 157
audience appeal 73-74
Augustine 29
authority x, 6-7, 24, 88
autonomy 9-10, 63

Bach, J. S. 25, 29, 46, 49, 78, 120, 135-36

Bahm, Archie 19
balance 10, 16, 40, 94
balance, directional. *See* directional balance
balance of emotion and reason. *See* emotion and reason, balance of
banality 22–23, 69, 77, 86, 127, 140, 148, 164
Barber, Samuel 120
Beaumont, Geoffrey 83
beauty 2–4, 18, 24, 30, 71, 92, 140, 142, 144
beauty, natural 18
becoming the *imago Dei* 32, 34, 36
Beethoven, Ludwig van 25, 29, 135
behavior, music as 47
believing, act of 93
Berdyaev, Nicolas 34
Berlinski, Herman 102, 136
Bernstein, Leonard 84
best, giving one's. *See* stewardship, principle one
Bible. *See* Word of God
biblical authority 6–7
Bonaventure 29
Bonhoeffer, Dietrich 41
Booth, Ballington 25
Bornkamm, Heinrich 115, 124
Brahms, Johannes 120
Broadway 82
Brunner, Emil 13, 123, 141, 143
business influence 75, 78. *See also* commercialization
Byrd, William 120

Calvin, John 28
CCM (Contemporary Christian Music) 24, 67–68, 75, 79, 121, 167
chant. *See* Gregorian chant
chaos 11–12, 22, 30, 162
Charismatics 92
children, music and 77, 117
choice 1–2, 25, 77, 81, 89, 105
choir ix, 1, 32, 113–15, 158–59
chorale 78, 121
church and pop music 76–79. *See also* popular music

church music as gospel analogy. *See* analogue of the gospel, music as
church music, contemporary situation ix, 6, 21, 23, 26, 36–38, 76–77, 85–86, 102, 109, 151, 154–55, 162, 165
church music education 119–22
church music program 15, 17, 19–26, 32, 36–38, 42–43, 46, 54–56, 79, 104, 119–22, 135–37, 144–45, 151–68
church music, quality of 21–23, 31, 35–38, 78–79, 112, 144–45, 162, 165
church musician as teacher 104, 121
church profile 153–55
church transcends culture 61–62
clergy. *See* pastors
cliché 20, 70, 74, 85–86, 103, 127, 129, 140, 164
coherence, aesthetic 11–12, 52, 130, 162
Coleridge, Samuel 18
commercialism, absence of 82
commercialization 13, 24, 37, 62–66, 69–70, 73–75, 78, 85–86
communication 5, 44–47, 50–53, 81, 125
communication, explicit (direct) 52–53, 56
communication, implicit (indirect) 40, 52–55
complacency, evaluative 20–21
complexity, compositional 74, 83, 95
composer 9 , 17–18, 26, 74, 78, 90, 95
composition 17–18, 40, 75, 95–95, 101, 111–12, 129–31, 133–34, 139
conditioning in worship 5, 98
conformity, evaluative 20–21, 64
congregation ix-x, 1, 32, 42, 112–14, 116–19, 121, 152
congregational musical profile 49–50, 96,114, 119–20, 149, 151, 153–55, 157

congregational progress 88, 105, 151, 153, 155, 157, 160

consecration. *See* attitude

contemporary Christian music. *See* CCM

contemporary culture and popular music 56-86, 119, 154

content, types of 51-52

contextualization x, 144, 147

continuity, aesthetic 52, 130

contrafacta 68

contrapuntal method 10, 122, 145-51, 151-68

contrapuntal tension 7, 10, 14, 62, 67, 122, 147-49, 151

Copland, Aaron 91-92

1 Corinthians 1:10 154

1 Corinthians 13:4-8 157

1 Corinthians 15:3, 17 138

counterpoint x-xi, 7, 40, 46, 67, 121-22, 147, 150-52, 156, 168

counterpoint, definition of 146

country music 67-68

craftsmanship 18-19, 22-25, 95, 111, 136, 141-42, 148, 161

Crashaw, Richard 40

creatio continua 12-13, 15-17, 36, 107, 109, 162

creatio ex nihilo 12

creation mandate 12-15, 17, 20-22, 26-28, 36, 58, 107, 132, 148, 161

creative process and phases 10, 17-19

creativity 10, 14-15, 17, 20, 24-31, 34-35, 37, 58, 72, 74-75, 83, 86, 88, 107-8, 127, 136, 139, 142-43, 145, 148, 151, 161, 163-65

creativity, definition of 17-18, 31, 35, 58

creativity, doctrine of 8-27, 37, 40, 142-43, 161-63

creativity, nurture of 19-21

creativity of God 8-9, 11, 29, 58, 162

Crouch, Andrae 49

crucifixion 58, 138-41, 144-46, 152

cultural determinism and conditioning 48, 50

cultural mandate 13-17, 19-21, 26, 43, 132, 161

culture x, 1, 13-14, 22, 34, 38, 43-44, 48-49, 62-63, 66, 86, 94, 114, 119, 153, 155

culture, contemporary. *See* contemporary culture

culture, post-Christian 38

Davison, Archibald T. 95, 135

delayed gratification 71, 79, 100-104, 148-49, 166

dependence 9-10, 22, 107, 146, 148

Dionysius 98

directional balance 146-47, 151-53, 159-60, 168

discipleship 58-59, 75, 108

discipline 6, 18, 59, 61-62, 71, 79, 102-3, 113, 134, 139, 140-42, 152, 165

disobedience 31, 81. *See also* fall, the

Distler, Hugo 49, 167

doing one's best (stewardship, principle one) 110-15, 121, 158

dominance, aesthetic 52, 131, 135

dominion-having 12, 23, 27-28

drums 54

Dyke, John 128

dynamic flexibility 15, 33, 40, 49, 55, 147, 152

Eliot, T. S. 16

emotion and reason, balance of 90-94, 98, 104-5, 148, 163

emotion and reason, imbalance of 88, 90, 94- 99

emotionalism 71-72, 97, 163-64

ends justify means 80-81

entertainment 13, 45, 49, 54, 59, 62, 68, 71-72, 75, 78-79, 81, 84, 97-98, 116, 136, 145, 148

escapism and fantasy 18, 60, 72-73, 97

eschatology 99-104, 102

Evangelicals 86, 91-92

evangelism, unprincipled 23-24, 80-81

evolution, artistic 16–17
excellence, aesthetic 18, 31–32,
    37, 73, 137, 148, 151, 158, 165
exodus, the 138

faith (and knowledge) 47, 87–105
faith action 87, 99–105, 148,
    166–67
faith, definition of 87
faith, the life of 87–99, 104–5,
    148, 163–64
faithfulness 108, 111–12
fall (the) 10, 14, 24, 28, 31–32,
    34, 36, 39, 50, 80–81, 113
Farmer, Herbert W. 88
folk music 77, 81–83
form and content 40, 45, 50–52,
    55–56, 69, 164–6 5, 168
form, musical 10–11, 19, 22–23,
    26, 30, 40, 46, 67, 149, 165
freedom 9–11, 21–22, 27, 30, 57–58,
    142. See also independence
French Ars Nova 95

Gaither, Bill 75, 120
Galiot, Johannes 95
general revelation 134, 165
Genesis 12
Genesis 1:26–27 29
Gilkey, Langdon 8
goal-inhibiting, aesthetic 100–104
God as mystery 123–37
God, creator and owner 107–9
gospel analogue and witness. See
    analogue of the gospel
gospel characteristics and traits x,
    5, 56–62, 75–76, 85–86
gospel content and meaning 52,
    54–55, 57, 81, 86, 154
gospel song and gospel music 67,
    76–79, 86, 121, 140
gospel, tenor of 57, 61–62
grace 57, 106, 113, 144, 152
grace, cheap 61
grace, costly 61
Great Commission 38, 67, 154
Gregorian chant 56, 83, 167
growth 3, 48, 110, 115–19, 121,
    148, 155, 159–60, 168. See also
    stewardship, principle two

Hanslick, Eduard 91
harmony 146–47
Harris, Roy 82
Haydn, Franz Joseph 128
Hayes, Mark 120
Hebrews 11:1 166
Hebrews 11:8–9 99
Hebrews 13:15 159
hedonism 14, 49, 54, 62–63, 71,
    98, 102, 154
heresy 3, 46
Higgs, James 95
Hindemith, Paul 65, 69, 91, 92, 96
historical heritage 15–17, 39, 64,
    88, 138, 154, 163
Hodeir, André 83
Hoffer, Charles 90
holiness 24, 124–25, 136–37, 167
holism 11, 58, 70, 87–89, 91, 94
Horsley, Imogene 95
humble exaltedness 10, 107, 148
humility 10, 40–45, 54–55, 107,
    139, 146, 148, 156–57, 162

idolatry 3–4, 7, 98
imagination 18–24, 31, 35, 58,
    70, 130, 142–45, 148, 161–63
imaging God 33–36, 164
imago as creativity 28–32
imago Dei 17, 27–38, 58, 132,
    143, 148
imago Dei, broad 28–32, 36, 38,
    161, 163
imago Dei, deformed 28
imago Dei, narrow 28, 32–38,
    61, 107–8, 164
imbalance, emotional and intellec-
    tual 94–99
immanence 7, 12, 39–40, 45, 149,
    167
immanence, radical 40, 125, 167
immediate gratification 63, 69,
    71, 75, 81, 102–4, 167
incarnation 7, 39–55, 93, 138,
    142, 149, 156, 158, 161–64
incarnation, artistic 14, 19, 30,
    40, 45
incarnation, form and content
    50–52, 149, 165

incarnation, humility 40-44, 148, 156-58
incarnation, implicit communication 52-54, 149
incarnation, relevance 44-50, 149, 165
independence 9-10, 22, 146-47, 152
infantilism 73, 116, 140
integrity xi, 5, 18, 21-26, 31, 35, 52, 54, 58-60, 70, 72, 74, 82-84, 127, 141, 148, 150, 152, 165
intellect 43, 71, 91-92. *See* music, emotion, and intellect
intuition 19, 22, 24, 40, 95, 133, 142-43

jazz 81, 83-85
John 13:8,14-15 157
John 13:13-15 41
Jones, W. Paul 34
joy 59, 75, 145
Judas 80, 81
judgment, aesthetic 24-26, 129-32
judgments, objective 5-6, 112, 121, 148, 159-60, 161-62
judgments, subjective 5, 112, 121, 148, 160
justification of means and ends 80-81

Kidner, Derek 118
Kierkegaard, Søren 128
kingdom-building 106
kitsch 63, 67, 71
knowledge precedes faith 47
Kodály, Zoltán 120
Korb, Arthur 73
Kuyper, Abraham 132

Lang, Paul Henry 89
Langer, Susanne 135
language 11, 47, 125, 133-34
law and legalism xi, 3, 59, 88-89, 106, 113, 152
Lewis, C. S. 72
life processes (in music) 14, 130-34

liking 120
listening and listener 9, 26, 38, 72, 90, 92, 96, 103, 111, 118, 120, 140
literalism (in painting) 126
Livingstone, Biganess 126
love 11, 30, 40, 43-44, 59-60, 62, 108, 158. *See also agape* love
Lovelace, Austin 135
Luke 22:26 157
Luther, Martin 68, 107, 116, 117, 123

manipulation 53-54, 97-98
market manipulation 64-66, 70
marketing 37-38, 52-53, 62, 64-65, 73, 78
marketing techniques 5, 53-54, 73
mass production 58, 69, 74, 85
materialism 14, 58, 62, 64, 85, 154
Matthew 5-7 61
Matthew 5:16 33
Matthew 25:14-19 110
maturation. *See* growth
maturation, musical and spiritual 79, 99, 104, 115-16, 147, 150, 164
maturity 3, 25, 97, 102-3, 115, 117, 149, 160, 163, 167
McLuhan, Marshall 57
meaning and music 11, 18, 47, 127, 134
means and ends 5
mediocrity 20, 26, 31, 36-37, 73, 75, 111, 114, 144, 164
medium and message 5, 46, 50-53, 56-57, 69, 76, 81, 86, 154, 165
melodic counterpoint 146-47, 156
Mendelssohn, Felix 120
merchandising. *See* commercialization
Messiaen, Olivier 167
methodology 7, 51, 56, 59, 80-81
Meyer, Leonard 101-2
mission, church 15, 77
model, music ministry 156-68
Moses 80-81
motivation 11, 59-60, 122

Mozart, Wolfgang Amadeus 120
MTV 85
multiculturalism. *See* pluralism
music and mystery 125–27, 133–34
music education 115–19, 119–21, 160–61
music, emotion and intellect in 91–99
music, meaning of. *See* meaning
music ministry, philosophical foundation 148. *See* philosophy
"music of the spheres" 142
music, sacred and secular 88–89, 104
musical analogue of the gospel. *See* analogue
musical imaging 32–36, 164
musical situationalism. *See* situationalism
musician as athlete 118
Muzak 65–66, 93, 128
mysterium tremendum 135, 137, 167
mystery and awe 44, 123–37, 167
mystery in worship 135–37

Nathan, Walter 136
natural world 10–12, 15, 18, 22
naturalism 14, 34
Nevin, Ethelbert 103
newness 23–24, 58
nihilism 11, 141
norms, artistic and musical 3, 161–62
numinous 124, 133, 136–37, 167
nurture, musical 19–22, 163

obedience 25, 33, 108
objective musical standards ix, 5–6, 111–12, 120–22, 148, 162
objectivity 3, 62, 150
omnipotence 123
omnipresence 123
omniscience 123
order 11, 18, 22
opposites. *See* tension of opposites
organic unity 51, 128–30
originality 30, 142
Otto, Rudolf 124
oughtness 48

painting 52, 126
parable of the Talents 110–15
paradox 7, 40, 67, 99, 145–46, 152, 168
Parker, DeWitt 3
pastor ix, 1, 152
pastoral music ministry x–xi, 1, 7, 10, 43–45, 50, 54, 63, 75, 86, 111, 122, 125, 132, 138–39, 147–48, 150, 156, 166, 168
Paul 15, 46, 80, 141, 153, 157
Pavlovian manipulation 98
Pentecostals 92
performer 9, 26, 111, 114, 139
performing 31, 40, 73
personality and personhood 9, 27, 30, 64
Peter 15
Peterson, John 120
Philippians 2:5–8 157
Philippians 4:8 52
philosophical coherence, comprehensiveness, and creativity 2, 6
philosophy ix–x, 1–4, 6–7, 148, 150
Pilate 128
pilgrimage 22, 33, 102, 115–16, 147–48, 166
Pinkham, Daniel 75, 120
Piston, Walter 147
Plato 127
pluralism, egalitarianism, and multiculturalism x, 14, 85, 152
pop culture and the church 37, 66, 80, 86, 141, 162, 165
pop music characteristics 62, 64, 67–76, 85–86
pop musicians 37, 78
popular, definition of 68
popular culture 21, 23, 62–80, 114, 153, 165
popular music 14, 23–24, 48–50, 56, 62, 72–73, 76–79, 97, 102–3, 136, 149, 161
Portnoy, Julius 95
post-Christian culture 38, 85, 165
practicality xi, 1, 6
pragmatism 2, 4–7, 78, 80–81, 121, 149, 151–52
pride 31, 42–43

progress, musical. *See* congregational progress
propaganda 52-54, 56
prophet, artist as 13
prophetic music ministry x, 1, 15, 48, 50, 62-63, 66, 69, 79, 147, 150, 155-56, 159, 166, 168
psychological conditioning 5, 98
psychological depression 115, 122
publishing 31, 37, 79
purpose 11-12, 18

quality, musical and artistic 5-6, 72-73, 80, 84, 88-89

Radcliff, H. 65
radical immanence. *See* immanence, radical
Rahner, Karl 108
RCP (religious commercial pop) 75
reality 72
reason 27, 30, 92, 148
redeemed imaging 34-38
redemption 28, 32, 34, 38, 47, 50, 143-46
reflection ix
regeneration 27, 61
relativism x, 6, 14, 62-64, 67, 85, 154, 162
relevance, extreme 47, 50
relevance, musical 40, 44-48, 54-55, 57, 63, 67, 149, 162
relevance, responsible 50
relevance, verbal 46-48
relevancy 44-50, 54, 149, 157
religion, emotion and intellect in 91
Renoir, Auguste 19
renunciation discipline 139-40, 144
responsibility 9, 12-13, 22, 30, 33, 106-8, 117
restraint 103
resurrection 58, 138, 141-46, 152
revolution, artistic 64
rhythm 54, 129
rock music 23, 46, 67-69, 72-73, 77, 97, 140
romanticism 60, 72, 75

Routley, Erik 7, 83, 140, 153
Ruskin, John 109

sacred and secular 88-89, 104
sacrifice 61, 75, 113, 139, 141
Sankey, Ira 120
Sapphira 58
Sayers, Dorothy 29
Schenker, Heinrich 100
Seay, Albert 95
security seeking 100, 104, 166
Seerveld, Calvin 43, 132
Selesses, Jacopin 95
self-acceptance 111
selfism and egocentrism x, 31, 49, 58, 62-63, 85, 98, 154
sensationalism 60, 73, 75
sentimentality 73, 97, 137, 140
servanthood 41, 43-44, 58, 61, 148, 156-57, 162, 168
simplicity, artistic 74, 83
singing 22, 32, 113, 145, 152, 159
situationalism, musical 147, 150, 152, 168
sloth, musical 31, 72, 112
Sousa, John Philip 56
sovereignty, human 10
sovereignty, of God 80-81, 101, 110
specialization, compositional 70
spiritual formation 66
Stainer, John 120
standards x, 24, 38, 50, 59, 64, 69, 75, 113, 117-18
standards, musical ix, 1, 14-15, 23, 42-43, 55, 65, 68, 89, 109, 112, 151
standardization 64, 127, 129
standardization, compositional 70-71
status quo 116
stewardship 106-22, 161, 163
stewardship, doing one's best, principle one 60, 75, 110-15, 148, 158-59
stewardship, growth, principle two 110, 115-19, 148, 159-60
stewardship, motivations for 106-7, 122
Stravinsky, Igor 91

style, musical   x, 46, 49, 69, 76, 88-89, 100, 161
stylistic unity   68
subjectivity   x, 5, 94, 98, 112, 121-22, 150
sui generis   (unique)   9
symbols, language   79, 133-34
symbols, musical   79, 134

talent(s)   110, 122, 158-60
taste   x, 1, 3, 20, 24, 38, 43, 46, 49, 50, 63-64, 93, 118, 122, 147, 154, 162
teachable spirit   118, 120
teaching ministry   104-5, 121, 166-68
technology   63-64, 66, 68, 75, 85-86
temporality   39, 130, 142-43
tendency gratification   52, 99-104, 166
tension of opposites   7, 10, 14, 62, 67,122, 130-31, 134, 145-49, 151
text   57, 135
theism   xi, 13-14, 154, 165
theology   ix-x, 7-8, 56, 109, 125, 145, 147, 150
theory, twentieth-century musical   75, 119, 167
time   130, 142
Tin Pan Alley   67, 69, 70
Top 40   73
tradition   17
transcendence   3,7, 40, 45, 123-25, 136-37, 149, 167
transience   60, 73, 75
travail   139, 141
triviality   31, 64, 85, 144
Trueblood, Elton   6
truth   x-xi, 7, 21, 30-31, 56-57, 62, 64, 80, 125, 133-35, 140, 147, 162, 165, 168
truth and musical composition   5, 54-55, 79, 127-34, 136-37, 149

uniqueness   9, 30, 57, 58
unity and variety   130-31,134

unity, artistic   90, 94
unity of life   87-88, 90, 94
universal artistic norms   3, 161
universal artistic principles   52, 129-31, 136
universality   57
utilitarian music   82

value   x, 1, 5, 14, 24-25, 38, 120, 132, 151
value, musical and artistic   54, 71, 73, 89, 101, 103-4, 136, 162
value system   ix, 1, 7, 62
valuing   120
variety   46, 53, 130, 147, 162
Vaughn Williams, Ralph   120
Victoria   120
Victorian church music   97, 140
vision   13-15, 30, 51, 102, 151
vocation of believer   108-10

Welk, Lawrence   49
Wentz, Frederick K.   109
western culture   93-94
wholeness   11, 58. See holism
widow's mite   60
Wilder, Amos   140
Willoughby, David   65
witness   34, 66-67, 69, 95, 117, 155
witness, direct   47
witness, musical   31-34, 36, 42, 46, 49, 52, 54, 56-57, 79, 81, 100, 164
witness, negative musical   38
Word of God   x-xi, 6-8, 26, 34, 40, 48, 60, 81, 121, 132-34, 145, 147-48, 151-52, 168
worldview   ix-xi, 6, 14, 46, 49, 63, 68-69, 71, 87, 89, 104, 154, 162
worldview, absurdist   162
worldview, theistic   xi, 13-15, 23, 102, 128, 154, 165
worship   4, 45-46, 50, 92, 94, 97-98, 100, 102, 116-17, 135-37, 145, 148, 163-64
worship, idolatry in   98
worth, musical and artistic   11, 101, 103
writing, linear   156